"Extraordinary tales about an ext
on a different facet of Monika Hel...,
The effect is that of a stained glass window, with light shining through in
myriad colors. Read it and laugh, weep, be inspired. Above all, take courage
that such a life has been lived among us."

— Elizabeth A. Johnson, CSJ
Distinguished Professor of Theology
Fordham University

"In these seven essays the shards of a life of a remarkable pioneering woman
theologian, teacher, administrator, poet, and mother take form revealing
the expansive Christian commitment to which each of us is called.
Sophisticated yet humble, learned yet generous and accessible, Monika
Hellwig was driven by a bedrock faith to serve God and her fellows. She
found her vocation at the intersection of her own unique capabilities and
the world's great needs. She was as Ireneaus allowed: a human fully alive and
hence the glory of God."

— Dana Greene
Author of *Evelyn Underhill: Artist of the Infinite
Life* and *The Living of Maisie Ward*

"William James wrote that saints are 'clearers of the darkness . . . vivifiers
and animaters of potentialities of goodness which but for them would be
forever dormant.' Monika sought to communicate theological truth to the
people of God while living out her vocation as mother, teacher, and spiritual
guide. She cleared the darkness of our minds and animated the good in
many she met. This powerful collection of essays shows the heroic virtues of
a remarkable woman, the people's theologian. Her story is ably told by the
cloud of witnesses who contribute their insights to this book."

— Terrence W. Tilley
Avery Cardinal Dulles, SJ, Professor
of Catholic Theology
Chair, Theology Department
Fordham University

Monika K. Hellwig

The People's Theologian

Edited by
Dolores R. Leckey and Kathleen Dolphin

A Michael Glazier Book

LITURGICAL PRESS
Collegeville, Minnesota

www.litpress.org

A Michael Glazier Book published by Liturgical Press

Cover design by David Manahan, OSB

© 2010 by Order of Saint Benedict, Collegeville, Minnesota. All rights reserved. No part of this book may be reproduced in any form, by print, microfilm, microfiche, mechanical recording, photocopying, translation, or by any other means, known or yet unknown, for any purpose except brief quotations in reviews, without the previous written permission of Liturgical Press, Saint John's Abbey, PO Box 7500, Collegeville, Minnesota 56321-7500. Printed in the United States of America.

1   2   3   4   5   6   7   8   9

Library of Congress Cataloging-in-Publication Data

    Monika K. Hellwig : the people's theologian / edited by Dolores R. Leckey and Kathleen Dolphin.
      p. cm.
    "A Michael Glazier book."
    ISBN 978-0-8146-5696-9 — ISBN 978-0-8146-5730-0 (e-book)
    1. Hellwig, Monika.   2. Catholic Church—Doctrines.   3. Christianity—Philosophy.   I. Leckey, Dolores R.   II. Dolphin, Kathleen.
  BX4705.H4625M66 2010
  230'.2092—dc22   2009052627

Contents

Preface

A unique bond between Monika and Saint Mary's College began with her formal inauguration of the college's Center for Spirituality in March 1985.

The Center began as an idea that, in the spring of 1983, I suggested to Dr. William Hickey and Dr. John Duggan, vice president/dean of faculty and president, respectively, of the college. At the time I was a faculty member at Marquette University. In interviews with these two officers of the college, it became clear that they were intent on regaining and highlighting the Catholic character of the college. The questions they posed to me: what can Saint Mary's, as a Catholic college for women, do to counteract the secularization of Catholic higher education, and, on the positive side, how can the college with its strong academic standards be an effective leader in Catholic higher education for women?

I suggested that Saint Mary's might well build on its unique heritage as a women's college under the sponsorship of the Congregation of the Sisters of the Holy Cross. Sr. Madeleva Wolff, CSC, president of the college from 1934 until 1961, instituted at Saint Mary's the pioneering Graduate School of Sacred Theology (1943–1970). This program granted doctoral and master's degrees in theology. This venture was then the only place where Catholic women could study graduate theology.

In the early 1980s, the women's movement in North America was gaining momentum. The Sisters of the Holy Cross who sponsor the college had in the era following Vatican II initiated summer programs for the spiritual enrichment of women religious. The convergence of the contemporary women's movement and the intense interest in spirituality made a women's college like Saint Mary's a likely and promising place for a Center for Spirituality, with a focus on the formation of women as leaders in the church and in society. President John Duggan and Vice President William Hickey instructed me to draw up plans for a Center for Spirituality, which I presented to the board of regents, now the board of trustees, in March of 1984. The board of regents immediately and enthusiastically endorsed it and within a week the administration of the Congregation of the Sisters of the Holy Cross made a significant financial contribution to it.

In the proposal was the establishment of an annual lecture on a theme concerning "Christian Spirituality, especially as this theme relates to women of the Church." Each lecturer was to prepare a text that would be available in published form the night of the lecture. Fr. Kevin A. Lynch, CSP, president and editorial director of Paulist Press from 1968 to 1998, agreed to publish annually what came to be known as the Madeleva Lecture series—published lectures that have had phenomenal success. These lectures are a major contribution to the spirituality of Christian women; they are composed and delivered by a "who's who" of prominent post–Vatican II Christian women.

It was now time to inaugurate formally the newly established Center for Spirituality and the Madeleva Lecture series. Not just any woman would do. With conviction in our choice, we turned to Monika Konrad Hellwig. Monika had been teaching theology at Georgetown University in Washington DC since 1967 and held the rank of full professor from 1977. She had been honored with the John Courtney Murray Award by the Catholic Theological Society of America in 1984. Monika had become a prolific author of incisive books and articles that featured a rare gift: she plumbed the depths of Catholic doctrine and yet presented her ideas in clear and compelling language.

Monika Hellwig delivered the first Madeleva Lecture in Spirituality on a stormy spring evening, March 23, 1985, to a very large crowd in the college's spacious O'Laughlin Auditorium. After the lecture Monika graciously autographed copies of the lecture, published by Paulist Press and entitled *Christian Women in a Troubled World*. This following notation appeared facing the title page: "This 1985 Madeleva Lecture celebrates the opening of the Center for Spirituality of Saint Mary's College, Notre Dame, Indiana, and honors the memory of the woman who inaugurated the college's pioneering program in theology, Sister Madeleva, C.S.C." Monika's lecture was received with great enthusiasm. On the following day, Sr. Franzita Kane, CSC, a long-time distinguished professor of English at the college, wrote to say: "Congratulations on your choice of the speaker to open the Center for Spirituality. No words are adequate to praise Monika Hellwig's address, nor the importance of her development of the subject. The quiet and understated dignity of the details, from your poster's presentation through the closing presentation, were all such as Sr. Madeleva would have approved, yet also in the best sense of the contemporary. Thanks for having the address printed."

Monika returned to campus for the fifteenth anniversary of the inaugural Madeleva Lecture, when all but one of the Madeleva lecturers to date gathered for a grand reunion called "Convergence 2000." At that time—on April 29, 2000, the feast of Catherine of Siena, saint and Doctor of the Church—these Madeleva lecturers composed and issued "The Madeleva Manifesto: A Message of Hope and Courage." The virtues of hope and courage aptly describe the message that Monika Hellwig spoke about and wrote about incessantly with never a lost step in a life that was marked with an uncommon vitality and enduring commitments. No woman has epitomized what it means to be hopeful and to act courageously more than Professor Monika Hellwig. Saint Mary's College will forever recall with gratitude that this gifted and courageous woman graced the first public event of the college's Center for Spirituality.

Keith J. Egan

Acknowledgments

This biography of Monika K. Hellwig is truly a collaborative effort. The Woodstock Theological Center at Georgetown University and the Center for Spirituality at Saint Mary's College at Notre Dame, Indiana, together conceived the project and brought it to fruition. In addition to the time and talent of Sr. Kathleen Dolphin, PBVM, director of the Spirituality Center, Saint Mary's provided the funding for the book. It also hosted a symposium where the authors presented their particular contributions to the book, *The People's Theologian*. The Woodstock Theological Center was represented in the project by senior fellow Dolores R. Leckey.

In a very real sense the book can be called a *collaborative biography* because each of the seven authors wrote from intimate knowledge of some aspect of Monika Hellwig's life. Their labors were motivated by deep respect for Monika and the desire to share her story far and wide. Woodstock and Saint Mary's are grateful for their early and continuing commitment to this project.

We have been blessed with the editorial and technical expertise of Paula Minaert in all phases of actually bringing the book into being. She is a gift to the publishing world.

Finally, Liturgical Press believed in the book when it was still an idea coming to life. We are grateful for the enthusiastic guidance of Hans Christoffersen, editorial director at Liturgical Press, which has carried us through to this moment. We are delighted that the book bears the Michael Glazier imprint. Michael was an important figure in Monika's life.

Introduction

Monika K. Hellwig: The People's Theologian is the story of a woman whose life spanned two continents and two centuries and who was formed by two of the major events of the twentieth century: World War II and the Second Vatican Council.

She was born in the German town of Breslau, the eldest of three girls of mixed ancestry, Jewish and Catholic. As anti-Semitism grew in Germany, Monika's mother sought refuge for her daughters and herself in the Netherlands. (Monika's father had died earlier in an auto accident.)

When war actually broke out, Monika and her sisters (Marianne and Angelika) were sent to Scotland and England for safety and for education. An unexpected gift was the experience of a loving foster family, which proved formative for them. The Hellwig girls were "rescued" from boarding school to live in the care and companionship of Barrett and Winefride Whale, both of whom were professors. Later Monika wrote about these generous people: "If a council of wise and compassionate men and women had searched all over England and Scotland they could not have found a better set of second parents for us than Barrett and Winefride Whale."[1]

Away from homeland and home, Monika learned at an early age that her personal experience was valid knowledge. This became the foundation of her life, and in particular of the integrity of her vocation as a theologian.

---

1. Monika K. Hellwig, "The Mandalas Do Not Break: A Theological Autobiographical Essay," in *Journeys*, ed. Gregory Baum (Mahwah, NJ: Paulist Press, 1975), 133.

The Jesuit Bernard Lonergan was one of the first theologians to recognize that God's revelation is embedded in the personal narrative. The concrete stories of women and men carry within them the traces of the divine. As we come to know flesh-and-blood people in all their mystery, and all their ordinariness, we come to know more of the Creator and Redeemer and Sustaining Spirit. So it is with Monika Hellwig, whose story is told in these pages by men and women who knew her well in the many roles that constituted her rich life lived in response to the Gospel. As the Carmelite poet Jessica Powers noted, to live in the Spirit of God is to be a listener.[2] Monika listened deeply and well. She first heard the Spirit's call as a vocation to the Medical Mission Sisters. Then, inspired by the teachings of the Second Vatican Council and her own introduction to the world of theology, she encountered a different but fully authentic call, to live the life of a layperson as envisioned by the council. All the evidence points to her free embrace of the vocation rising within her. Everything that followed in her life—her academic work, her career as a teacher and later an administrator, becoming a single parent of adopted children, her insertion into communities that nurtured lay life (her parish and a prayer group modeled on the Jesuit Christian Life Communities)—are all of a piece. She enacted the life of a committed layperson by fully participating in those expressions of the wider church. It was as if the documents of the Second Vatican Council animated her inner life.

When Sr. Kathleen Dolphin, PBVM, director of the Center for Spirituality at Saint Mary's College, Notre Dame, Indiana, and I were wondering how best to tell the story of Monika K. Hellwig, it came to us that many voices were needed. I thought of a story told by the memoirist and poet Patricia Hampl. It's a story about a bus ride—on a Greyhound bus—when Hampl saw a beautiful golden-haired young man bid a passionate good-bye to a rather plain middle-aged woman. The woman, wearing a flowered housedress that zipped up the front, boarded the bus and took her seat next to Hampl, clutching her bags piled high on her lap. After a few moments she turned to Hampl and said that everyone thinks, at first, that the god-like creature throwing kisses to the

---

2. Jessica Powers, "To Live with the Spirit," in *Selected Poetry of Jessica Powers*, ed. Robert Morneau and Regina Siegfried (Washington, DC: ICS Publications, 1999).

departing bus must be her son. But no, she continued, he's my husband; we're very happy. Then she added, almost to herself, "Oh, I could tell you stories." And then she fell asleep. The woman didn't say I *will* tell you stories, because, says Hampl, her story, their story, was too big for mere telling.[3]

One could say that about Monika's story. It is too much (as is usual with those who love well and deeply) for any one account. Something more is needed—many voices. And that is what we have rendered in this book, something like a choir of voices of people who knew Monika well in different facets of her life. The members of this assembled choir are, in truth, primary sources: they speak (or sing) of Monika from first-hand experience.

- Fr. Gerard Sloyan writes of meeting Monika when she began theological studies at The Catholic University of America as a Medical Mission Sister. That experience was an opening into what would later become a whole new life for Monika.

- Fr. William McFadden, SJ, who was head of the Georgetown University theology department in the late 1960s, hired her as the first woman to teach theology at Georgetown in what might be referred to as an act of faith. In a sense they were both pioneers.

- Undertaking this new and exacting job somehow led her into another aspect of her deepening lay vocation: motherhood. This important chapter by Evelyn Haught, who over the years was a close friend of Monika's, answers the question of why she undertook the major responsibility of motherhood.

- Monika was, by every account, a "master teacher" and one of her former students, Rosemary Carbine, now a theologian herself, writes about her effect on so many of her students and how unself-consciously she mentored them.

- Monika's role in bringing the Christian Life Community's method of prayer and faith-sharing to the Georgetown University campus is recounted by a member of that group, Lee Leonhardy, who also

---

3. Patricia Hampl, *I Could Tell You Stories: Sojourns in the Land of Memory* (New York: W.W. Norton & Co., 2000).

describes Monika's humble search for deeper commitment to the spiritual life.

- Chapter 6 describes what the author, John Haughey, SJ, refers to as Monika's *catholicity*. He sees her as a steward of the mysteries of God, one who is a leader of the People of God. She is a leader not by appointment or office or election but simply through the authenticity of her being. Honoring her theological achievements and intellectual competency, Fr. Haughey goes beyond these qualities to the gift of insight, which she shared generously with those around her.

- The final chapter, by Suzanne Clark, sketches Monika's life as a parishioner, in particular as a parishioner in the last parish to which she belonged, St. Rose of Lima in Gaithersburg, Maryland. Monika, like legions of laity, found the parish to be an anchor in what was sometimes a chaotic life. There she could offer simple service (like tending the garden) and receive the ministrations of the pastor and the pastoral team. In some ways the parish brought together the strands of her life.

One piece of Monika Hellwig's story is *not* included, namely the years when she served as executive director of the Association of Catholic Colleges and Universities (1996–2005). It was a time of tension in the U.S. church as college presidents and bishops grappled with the implications of *Ex Corde Ecclesiae*, especially in regard to academic freedom. At a later time, Saint Mary's College and the Woodstock Theological Center hope to facilitate a dialogue about her role as administrator and ambassador of Catholic higher education. This volume, however, highlights Monika as a premier lay theologian and as a model for commitment to the lay vocation.

The seven authors did not consult one another about their individual contributions. Yet we see some recurrent themes in the chapters: wisdom, pastoral sensitivity, her innate sense of nourishing, her intellectual rigor, her wholeness—a harmony in the choir. We also see in these pages how Monika incorporated her artistic, intuitive self into different parts of her life. She wrote poetry (and some of it you will find here); she wrote spiritual reflections; she spoke a language that could reach not only the realm of reason but also the realm of the heart, what

St. Ignatius of Loyola called *interiority*. That's what she brought to the people beyond the boundaries of the academy. Truly, Monika Hellwig was *The People's Theologian*.

Dolores R. Leckey, General Editor
Senior Fellow, Woodstock Theological Center

The communes that are religious communities sometimes work supremely well, and in the most tangible way provide eschatological witness. They demonstrate that neither possessions nor expertise, nor yet family connections, need be the basis for personal dignity or identity or relationship with others. Community is constituted by the simple will to accept others and to subordinate personal goals to the common goals. Because of my experiences of religious community life, the vision of the reign of God among men seems to be quite realistic and functional.

> — from "The Mandalas Do Not Break:
>   A Theological Autobiographical Essay"
>   by Monika K. Hellwig

Chapter 1

A Friend for Life

Gerard Sloyan

I first met Monika Hellwig in a classroom at The Catholic University of America in the fall of 1954. She was then Sister Mary Cuthbert of the Society of Medical Mission Sisters and fresh off the boat from Liverpool, having come to Washington DC from a house of formation of her congregation in South Shields in England. Accompanied by another sister, a Dutch woman, she had been sent to the States to earn a master's degree in religious studies. The academic department of religious education in the Graduate School of Arts and Sciences at CUA was the setting of a graduate course in the gospels in which she was enrolled. The students were five or six in number. Sister Cuthbert was alone among them in bringing to the first class her Greek New Testament. I later learned that she had earned a degree in law after secondary school, a European possibility that meant that she was twenty-one or so when she entered her religious community.

That community had been founded not far from the university in the Brookland area of Washington by Anna Dengel, an enterprising Austrian physician who had learned that Indian women in what was later the Republic of Pakistan could not be treated by male doctors. She decided to do something about it. Sister Mary Cuthbert might have thought that in joining this congregation she had embarked on a medical career, because professional health care was its work. But the initial studies in which she was enrolled as part of her formation as a member of her institute determined that her career was to be a theological one.

That year was my fifth on the university faculty, which I had joined at age thirty. The academic religious education department offered the undergraduate courses in the study of religion; all students (except

1

those in engineering, architecture, and nursing) were required to take eight semesters in this study. The department also had had MA- and PhD-granting power going back to the mid-1930s. There were no offerings in religious pedagogy, as the department's name might suggest, only biblical and formal theological studies. Nonclerics of both sexes were ineligible for pontifical (that is to say, Roman See-approved) degrees in the adjacent School of Sacred Theology. That might lead one to think that many sisters, brothers, and priests preparing to be college teachers of religion (a few were beginning to call it theology) were crowding the graduate school to prepare to teach in the colleges their diocese or congregation conducted. But this was not so.

Theology in Catholic colleges was being taught largely by regular and secular priests on the basis of their seminary education, while a few sisters and brothers with doctorates in philosophy or history were acting as instructors in religion. The significance of this situation for Sister Cuthbert was that the other candidates for the MA in the program were all engaged in high-school teaching. But not this lively, intellectual Englishwoman. She was being groomed for the small faculty of her congregation's school in the Fox Chase section of Philadelphia, which was teaching candidates at the college level through its relation to The Catholic University of America.

Sister Mary Cuthbert Hellwig completed the course work and wrote a thesis for the master's degree within a year and a summer and left Washington, to return for graduation the following June. It was not long before she was sent to the University of Notre Dame, over the course of five summers, for another master's degree, this time in the study of the liturgy. After that came some nondegree summer courses in linguistics at the University of Oklahoma, probably to give her a foundation in Urdu to be shared with the sisters she was teaching—because throughout all this time, Monika was on the faculty at Fox Chase. She was fast becoming a polymath. In the early years of her teaching she returned to Washington for a semester to sit in on one of my undergraduate courses for both its content and mode of presentation. I was humbled by her presence, for she was already a star. Seated in that assembly of youth, I recall, was a Jersey Cityite who had interrupted his college years to do his army service: Philip Bosco, later to be much employed on stage and screen. Seated next to him was a flaming redhead named Nancy Dunkle. Her later employment in life was to be mother of their seven children.

When the time came for Sister Hellwig (this term is much later Catholic vocabulary) to profess her final vows, she asked me to be the homilist at the public rite. I was pleased to be part of that happy day. Later, during or immediately after the four sessions of the Second Vatican Council, Monika in her position as dean of her small faculty—actually, director of studies—invited me to be one of several speakers to address the sisters who were at Fox Chase for their summer community days. She proposed for a topic any aspect of the sixteen documents promulgated by the 2,500-plus council fathers. My remarks were followed attentively by these intelligent women, especially the one on *Perfectae Caritatis* (28 October 1965), which was devoted to the renewal of the vowed life of men and women living in community. In the floor exchange that followed, the question of the religious habit was raised. I do not recall having spoken of it. Their congregation, the Medical Mission Sisters, wore a quite simple slate-gray dress belted in the same cloth with a blue, tending toward violet, veil over a starched linen cap pointed in front. I ventured the opinion that perhaps it was not wise to continue in this religious habit, not because it was obviously Christian in a Muslim sea but because it was Western. The memories of colonialism and the British raj were still very strong in the East. Better the sari and cloth pants beneath, I said, or whatever the dress of the local women. At that point the American superior of the congregation rose to chide me for presuming to make such a suggestion. She reminded me in vigorous terms "how much we love our habit," and any such proposed adaptation was ill-originated if it came from the council (it hadn't). As I was leaving, this good woman thanked me at the door for my service that day and Monika caught me as I walked to my car. She apologized gently for the vigor of the superior's response to my suggestion. I came away thinking that some of the decisions of the assembled bishops at the council, although not in that matter, were perhaps not so popular at Fox Chase 19111, headquarters of the Medical Mission Sisters.

Not long after that, Sister Mary Cuthbert was assigned to the staff of the general house in Rome with no time-consuming duties. She immediately joined a network of Americans there, among them some diocesan priests doing graduate studies, at Jesuit Fr. Riccardo Lombardi's Movement for a Better World center in Rocca di Papa, across Lake Albano from Castel Gandolfo. The movement engaged laypeople, religious sisters and brothers, secular and regular priests, and bishops, who try to serve the renewal/transformation of the whole Western church.

When I learned by correspondence of her relative liberty, I already was well aware of her gifts as an academic. So I asked the rector of The Catholic University of America to write a letter of invitation to Monika's major superior, asking that she be released for PhD studies with a view to serving on the CUA faculty. That was the way things worked in those days. If a school or department was interested in having a priest, sister, or brother leave one academic position for another in Washington, a letter would be sent to the person's bishop or religious superior. Normally the individual would not be sounded out for willingness. This was to avoid disappointment if the answer were no but, even more, to avoid the appearance of the individual scheming to leave the local scene if a college president did not want to see a gifted teacher depart. This arrangement seems fairly bizarre but that was the way it worked fifty years ago. In this case, it resulted in a negative response, rather sharply written. The large university preying on a very small congregation indeed!

But by that time Monika knew that the game was afoot. Some weeks later she wrote me a letter that was a complete surprise, saying that she was resigning from her sisterhood and asking if the offer were still open. It was, and she came. In a close-packed year of course and credit pursuit, the now Miss Hellwig added to the academic capital of her earlier MA studies and began to search out a dissertation topic. I missed at first-hand what followed because after twenty-one years of study and teaching at the university, interrupted by three years as a parish assistant in my diocese, I accepted with my bishop's permission a position at the Commonwealth-related Temple University in Philadelphia, named for its founder's church, the Baptist Temple.

In my first weeks there I learned from Monika of two important developments in her life. She had been accepted for dissertation direction by Professor Roger Balducelli, an Oblate of St. Francis de Sales, and she had applied for and been awarded a full-time appointment at Georgetown University. Her gender was a help in that, because the undergraduate college of the university, an all-Jesuit enterprise, had not long been coeducational in student body and instruction. Monika and a Protestant layman and shortly a rabbi chaplain-teacher in that department broke new ground.

I had come to know her in my last full-time year at The Catholic University of America in a graduate seminar populated by some highly gifted candidates for the PhD. The seminar took the form of an exposition of the masterwork of a variety of influential religious thinkers: Strauss, Feuerbach, James, and the like. One of Monika's two subjects that year was August Comte's *Système de politique positive*, which she dissected in elegant oral prose. I got to know well that year her giftedness, but above all her talent for friendship. My decision to bring her aboard as a CUA instructor was fully validated. When she wrote me in early fall of her move to Georgetown, she made clear that it was not a betrayal of trust but done out of economic necessity. She had to have a source of income after that first year's scholarship benefits ran out and her enrollment continued. It could have been extended a second year on its meager terms but two birds in the bush were better than a meager bird in hand. She had made the best of the present *kairós*, as Ephesians recommends.

I visited frequently with Monika during her early years at Georgetown, both in Philadelphia and Washington. Sometimes the visits were in writing—she was an excellent correspondent—and from them I learned of her hope to marry. She kept me abreast of one warm friendship but then fell silent when it came to nothing. It was probably at that point that she began to explore adoption possibilities, which worked out very well. I was invited to be the minister of baptism of her first child, Erica, in a Georgetown area church and began to receive reports of the joys of early motherhood. She also called on me for the sacramental celebration of her first son but when she adopted his brother (none of the three are birth siblings), I was not out of touch but I was off the East Coast. In all those years, Monika served regularly as a minister of the Mass on Sunday, first at Dahlgren Chapel of Georgetown University and later in the parish church of St. Rose of Lima in Gaithersburg. The clergy in both places were deeply appreciative of her sacramental participation, both for its dependability and her skill in the execution of various roles. Her long-term association with the priests of *La Compañia de Jesús* at her university resulted in a warm affection for them corporately. Once, when we served together on a committee of external evaluators of the theology department of another university conducted by the Jesuits, I tried in the framing of the final report to indicate several weaknesses. Monika would have none of it. The fathers could do no wrong.

Throughout her Georgetown University teaching years, which were close on thirty, this extraordinary woman was busy about two matters related to her classroom teaching but achieved apart from it. One was the publication of some twenty books. The first was *What Are the Theologians Saying?* in 1970. Monika had asked me to write a foreword to this book, which went into six printings within three years. One of her last books, *Guests of God: Stewards of Divine Creation* (2000), is concerned with the social morality of discipleship, including the demands of ecology, and is deftly illustrated by pen sketches done by her daughter Erica Hellwig Parker. All can be described as adult catecheses—popular theology, if you will—of the highest order. A number of the titles came into being through friendship with the Irish-born publisher whose firm bore his name, Michael Glazier. The editing of two collections under the latter imprint absorbed much of her energies in the 1970s and 1990s. Those collections were The Message of the Sacraments Series and The Theology and Life Series. Paulist Press also published some of Professor Hellwig's output, three titles in fact: *The Eucharist and the Hunger of the World*, *What Are They Saying About Death and Christian Hope?* and perhaps her most well received of all, *Understanding Catholicism*. The second extra-classroom activity was summer-session teaching in several locations, most often St. Michael's in Winooski, Vermont, an Edmundite Catholic College.

In the midst of all that, and the serious obligations of parenting her three adopted children, she managed to serve as the second woman president of the Catholic Theological Society of America (1986–1987), a position that is not honorary. The duties of the preceding year and the year of the presidency are not light. It may have been Monika's reception of the John Courtney Murray Award of that Society in 1984 that prompted the officers to put her name in nomination not long after. In any case, she won the office by elective vote.

When I came back to Washington after twenty-five years away, I expected to be in more regular touch with Monika and her family than when we were separated by one hundred and a quarter miles. I was present at Erica's wedding but there was not much socializing otherwise. Monika's resignation from the Georgetown faculty came in the spring before my beginning as an adjunct professor there, so regular contact on that campus was not to be. Her executive directorship of the Association of Catholic Colleges and Universities was fairly time-consuming and involved visits to member institutions in Europe, Asia, and Latin America. I stopped by once at the association's offices on Dupont Circle and found her in the midst of a few executive decisions about painting, carpeting, and plumbing. It was only when I attended a dinner held to honor her retirement from that highly responsible position that I learned from a number of spoken tributes how effective she had been in office—especially in conveying to the Roman See the difficulties large universities experience in retaining their Catholic character in exactly the ways expected by the curial authors of *Ex Corde Ecclesiae* (15 August 1990). That evening's celebration of Monika's skill in that position was the last time I was in her company. Neither of us, of course, could have imagined it to be such. But so it was when a legion of friends and admirers around the country and around the world learned of her relatively sudden departure from our midst. As Shakespeare said, "This fell sergeant, death, / is strict in his arrest."

Those who learn of a person's life and achievements either in print or by hearsay are inclined to say, inwardly, yes, but what was she like? Who was the person behind all this doing and achieving? Monika Hellwig was a loving, caring, frightfully intelligent woman of faith and action. She was matter-of-fact in speech and totally modest in bearing. Her accent had tones of her Liverpool upbringing, not Oxbridge, and the precise and moderately clipped speech of the British was Americanized slightly over the years. Her faith was, of course, trust, absolute trust in God's providence. It took the form of certainty that whatever needed to be done could be done. Many times she would mention in utter calm the latest challenge in the life of one of her children, something that might seem to an outsider impossible to cope with successfully. Not Monika. She carried on with a blessed assurance. All this is to say that she was a happily incurable optimist. At the same time, or as part of it, she was thoroughly charitable in speech, putting the best face possible on the actions of others. This did not mean, however, that she could not make critical judgments on such actions when necessary.

Monika was a serious person, not a jokester or loud laugher, which does not mean she could not see the fun in things. Her disposition was lively and upbeat, not dull or heavy. Above all, she was a faithful and true friend. The best way to sum it up is to say that, gifted by nature and grace, she was utterly faithful to the terms of her baptism in infancy as she came to know them. This made her a good and kind and thoughtful person, as it should any of us. Prayer was her secret. And her model, I suspect, though she never told me this, was Winefride Whale who, with her husband, had raised three little girls from Germany.

"Theology is the critique of praxis." When I first read those words in an essay by Gustavo Gutierrez, I recognized them immediately as a description of my own experience. Christian theology is the critique of the praxis of trying to live by the Gospel of Jesus Christ within a constantly changing world. Catholic theology is the critique of the praxis of doing it within the framework of the Catholic community and its traditions. Following through this line of thought, one also comes to the realization that there is indeed a characteristically lay theology, a characteristically feminine theology, and a characteristic theology of the uprooted, just as there is a characteristic and uniquely powerful theology that springs again and again from the bitterly oppressed and overwhelms us all from time to time in our comfortable entrenchments.

— from "The Mandalas Do Not Break:
A Theological Autobiographical Essay"
by Monika K. Hellwig

Chapter 2

Monika as Colleague

William C. McFadden, SJ

I n the spring of 1967 I received a letter from a graduate student at The Catholic University of America. It was typed on onionskin paper and the typist had such a forceful stroke that the letter *o* was regularly punched out, or else was left as what I later learned to call a "hanging chad."

She said that she was writing her dissertation but the school's library did not extend borrowing privileges to graduate students so she was exploring the possibility of teaching part-time at Georgetown University. Presumably, as a faculty member at another university, she could resolve that problem. She offered to teach a wide range of courses in systematic theology but had calculated she would need a stipend of at least $4,600.

At the time the theology department was all-male, mostly Jesuits with a few laymen. It was true that I was looking to hire some women theologians, and her suggested stipend was exceedingly modest, but we had already completed hiring for the coming academic year.

Before I got around to writing back to her, Walter Cook, a fellow Jesuit in the linguistics department, asked me if I was going to hire Monika Hellwig to teach theology. I remember his very words: "Because if you aren't, I will move heaven and earth to get her in the linguistics department." When Walter came to Georgetown to begin a doctoral program in the summer of 1962, Monika, then Sister Cuthbert, taught the introductory course. He informed me that on the basis of that one course, he had "coasted" to the doctorate.

That word *coasted* caught my attention. Walter was a genial fellow. We sang in a barbershop quartet together. But when it came to academics he was always deadly serious. He was telling me she was an extraordinary teacher. I immediately made an appointment with the academic vice president and, as he told me later, it was clear to him I was not going to leave his office until he authorized me to hire Monika Hellwig . . . for $4,600.

When she sent me her curriculum vitae as part of the formal hiring process, I quickly realized that (1) she was older than I (only four months older but from time to time over the years she would enjoy beginning a sentence with, "When you get a little older, you will realize that . . ."); (2) she was better educated (she had a law degree, a degree in social work, had done several years of graduate work in linguistics, and would soon have a doctorate in theology) and had taught at the college level longer than I; and (3) there was little hope we could retain her services in the future. We were at the time an undergraduate department, teaching required courses to Catholic students. We did not have a graduate program. We did not even have an undergraduate major.

Her future in the department, however, almost became a moot point. That winter I received a phone call from our hospital with the news that Monika was in the intensive care unit. She had stepped out from between two parked cars on Wisconsin Avenue and was knocked over by a passing motorist. When I got there, I was much relieved to find her sitting up in her hospital bed and in her usual cheery way she was putting everyone at ease. When I asked if she needed anything, she said she would appreciate it if I went to her apartment and picked up six items. She then gave me the precise location where each item might be found. I began to relax. She was fine.

She taught two courses in the fall of 1967 (Rahner and Theology of the Catholic Church) and two others the following spring (Revelation and Freedom and Theology of Freedom). I think I am responsible for those last two course titles. Freedom was very much in the air in those troubled times and I told her any course with *freedom* in the title attracted strong student interest.

While teaching four new courses that year, Monika also completed her dissertation and received her PhD in 1968 but, instead of going back to England as I anticipated, she agreed to teach for us full time the following year. We had begun to explore the possibility of starting a major in our department and she was so enthusiastic about the idea that we plunged ahead. Four brave students signed up for the program in the fall of 1968, and her contribution was to teach the course in systematic theology in the spring of 1969.

Sometime during that semester Monika invited me to dinner to meet two friends from graduate school, Jack and Evelyn Haught. Jack was finishing his degree in theology and expressed interest in teaching our introductory course, The Problem of God. On Monika's strong recommendation I went back to the academic vice president the next day and was authorized to invite Jack to join our department that fall.

In May 1970 those of us who lived on campus woke up to the sounds of police sirens and the smell of teargas. Thousands of students from across the country had come to Washington to shut down the government as a protest against the Vietnam War. They planned to block the bridges from Virginia so no one could come to work that day. Unfortunately for their plans, the police got up earlier than they did and prevented them from getting on the bridges. At Key Bridge on the District side, fights broke out and the police routed the demonstrators, who then fled to our nearby campus with the police in pursuit.

Soon the pastoral scene of Healy Lawn and Copley Lawn was covered with a haze of teargas and several dozen students lay on their backs while other students poured water in their reddened eyes. I phoned Monika and told her that all classes had been canceled and to stay away from campus. I had no idea how this was going to turn out. She agreed not to come but with some reluctance, I thought. I found out later that she had been following the story on the radio. To deal with the teargas, she had already prepared a large sponge soaked in witch hazel and packed it in a clear plastic case. Later she asked me with a mischievous twinkle in her eye if I had also called Jack Haught and told him to stay home. Thus did I learn that Monika felt quite capable of taking care of herself.

Around the same time Monika and a few other faculty members made a spiritual retreat and afterwards she decided it would be a good idea for them to get together each week during the semester for Mass and conversation. I was invited to join them and suggested that Copley Crypt would be the perfect place for Mass. Afterwards we could go to the student cafeteria, Marty's-on-the-Potomac, for lunch. For the first year or two I would prepare some ideas for reflection on the Scripture readings but soon Monika and a couple of others agreed to take over that role for this little community. Around that time the Jesuit community began to offer hospitality at meals in their dining room and I was able to reserve the guest dining room every Tuesday for our group. There is no doubt that Monika was the animating presence for this group of friends for over twenty-five years.

I remember another afternoon in the spring of 1970. While I was chatting with her at the end of the day, Monika happily announced that she was going to adopt a baby girl. I was taken completely by surprise. I didn't even know that it was possible for single persons to adopt babies but she of course had checked it out thoroughly. Then she delivered the clincher: "Why should a baby be raised in an institution if I can provide her with a loving home?"

She decided to name the baby Erica and with great enthusiasm she turned to the planning of Erica's baptism. She invited her mentor from Catholic University, Rev. Gerard Sloyan, to perform the ceremony. He was now at Temple University but would be delighted to drive to Washington for the grand occasion. I was honored to be asked to be the baby's godfather, but I did not know if that was permitted. A canon lawyer told me that I would incur an impediment against marrying Erica in the future. After a quick calculation of the age difference between us, I decided it was a risk I was willing to take. The baptism was scheduled to take place at Holy Trinity Church in Georgetown at five o'clock on Sunday, January 17, 1971.

Not being a football fan, Monika was unaware that was also the date of Super Bowl V. Our neighbors, the Baltimore Colts, were playing the Dallas Cowboys, the Washington Redskins' archrivals. Of course, in the great scheme of things a football game does not have the importance of a baby's baptism, but Catholics like to think of themselves as "both/and" people, i.e., when there are two good things, they choose both one and the other.

So, that afternoon I watched as much of the game as I could on television but neither team could seal the victory. I drove to the church and parked out front, still following the game on the radio. With the outcome still in doubt, the time had come to join the small crowd inside the church. I soon found out, though, that the celebrant had not yet appeared, so I solemnly signaled to Jack Haught and we went out to catch the end of the game on the car radio.

Three things happened in quick succession: the Colts intercepted a pass, they kicked a field goal to win by three points, and Fr. Sloyan's headlights appeared in my rearview mirror. Did he time his arrival so he could hear the end of the game? I have never had the courage to ask him, even though we have been teaching in the same department for the last ten years.

Monika adopted a second child, Michael, in 1974. In December, when Michael was about three years old, she invited me to join them in trimming their Christmas tree. On a previous occasion she had tried to get me to feed Erica in her high chair and the results were not pretty. "Now this," I thought, "this is something I am really good at." I remember when I was a child grabbing a handful of tinsel and throwing it at the sweet-smelling evergreen but my father patiently showed me how to take individual strands of tinsel and arrange them evenly on all the branches and then distribute the Christmas tree balls, with the larger ones toward the bottom of the tree and the smaller ones toward the top. I confidently waited for my chance to shine.

But it never came. Monika put out the materials and first Erica and then Michael took turns throwing bunches of tinsel in the general direction of the tree and attaching the ornaments in a haphazard fashion. The only thing they got right was the placement of the angel on the top of the tree, but there was some pretty obvious coaching from Monika on that one. Mostly, though, she just stood there and beamed at the sorriest-looking Christmas tree that I had ever seen. But, as she told me later, she wanted it to be *their* tree.

Even with a second child to care for, Monika still had the time and energy to plan a new interdisciplinary major program, Catholicism and Western Civilization. She recruited two colleagues from the history department and one from the philosophy department to serve as faculty for the program. One of the program's features was a seminar each semester that all four faculty members attended each week and that took up topics such as Symbols in Catholicism and Catholic Intellectual Life.

For Monika, the seminar was in addition to her regularly assigned classes. One of her colleagues, Tom McTighe of the philosophy department, was also teaching the seminar as an extra course. A couple of years later, I met him on the way to one of these two-hour sessions. I asked him how it was going and with just a touch of weariness he confided to me, "It's tough working for a saint!"

The Second Vatican Council introduced an extraordinary renewal of Catholic teachings and practices but it was all done much too quickly for many Catholics. They found themselves in the situation of Mary Magdalene, standing at the empty tomb and saying: "They have taken away my Lord and I know not where they have laid him." One of Monika's greatest gifts was her ability to encourage people to see that the changes could be looked at as an opportunity to deepen and enrich their practice of the faith.

In 1970 she had published her first book, *What Are the Theologians Saying?* Over the next twenty-six years she wrote many more books and about one hundred chapters and articles. While she was in our department, we did not have a graduate program, but in the summer she taught in the graduate programs at Notre Dame, San Francisco, Dayton, DePaul, and Princeton Theological Seminary. She was busy but not too busy to find the time to go through the process of adopting one more child and so Carlos joined the family in 1980.

Basketball fans will recall 1984 as the year the Georgetown Hoyas, led by Patrick Ewing, won the national championship. In the theology department we remembered it as the year when the Catholic Theological Society of America paid tribute to the career of Monika Hellwig. The president of the society, Leo J. O'Donovan, SJ, artfully wove together in his speech the titles of seven of Monika's books. He concluded by asking: "What are the Theologians Saying?" His reply to that question was that the theologians are saying "with pride and admiration and delight that we award our John Courtney Murray Medal for Distinguished Achievement in Theology" to Monika Hellwig, our deeply esteemed colleague.

When Monika first joined us, we all shared three offices in a Second World War barracks building that a clever president purchased for a dollar and had faced with bricks. We quickly outgrew that arrangement and in 1970 we moved to the O'Gara building, which had originally been a barn but was later converted to the student infirmary. In 1982 we were delighted to move into a new building, the Bunn Intercultural Center, but our stay there was rather brief. Our department continued to grow and so in 1987 we moved again to First New North, formerly a freshman dormitory, which had been completely renovated. The faculty was happy because they now had space for more books, filing cabinets, and a computer table. In what was probably a sign of the times for her, all Monika wanted was an easy chair. She told me she had found it increasingly necessary to take short naps during the day so I purchased for her one of those upholstered recliners in which you can get almost horizontal. I told her she really deserved one of those prestigious named chairs that other departments have—after all, she had been elected president of the Catholic Theological Society of America in 1986—but this was the best we could do. It was fitting that she was sitting in this chair in 1990 when I went down the hall to her office to tell her that the president had named her the Landegger Distinguished Professor of Theology, a title she held until she retired from the department in 1996.

As I look back over the twenty-nine years Monika spent with us in the theology department, I remember, of course, her many contributions to our program and to the life of the department. Mostly, though, when I think of her, busily engaged in the whirl of her many diverse activities, I remember her buoyant, irenic spirit.

I would like to conclude with a vivid example of that spirit in action. This has the advantage of giving her the last word, which I think she richly deserves. The last time I heard Monika speak in public was in 2001. It was a memorable occasion. The Catholic Common Ground Initiative sponsored a lecture on June 22 at Georgetown University by Cardinal Avery Dulles, SJ, with a response by Monika, who was then the Executive Director of the Association of Catholic Colleges and Universities. The title of the cardinal's talk was "Dialogue, Truth, and Communion."

Dulles presented the results of his impressive research into various forms of dialogue from the time of Plato to the present. He then distinguished between the nature of dialogue (1) within the church, (2) between the church and others, and (3) according to the "liberal model," which is based on an understanding that the intrinsic truth of moral and religious statements is not attainable, and therefore mutual tolerance is the highest possible goal.

Most of Monika's response consisted of an enthusiastic endorsement of his presentation. On one point, however, Monika wished to offer a "friendly amendment." In his first model, the dialogue within the church, Dulles understands the church as already having the truth and engaging in dialogue with others so that they may be led to the truth. Monika suggested that this model is fully appropriate only in a relatively small number of situations: namely, those that deal with matters that are of the essence of Christian life and faith. She further suggested that this model might be improved by including within it what she called the "collegial model" of coming to truth when dealing with all other matters.

She gave as examples of the collegial model the way of proceeding in the world of science and of advanced scholarship in any field. This model was also employed in the disputations of the medieval schools. The scholars put forward their arguments and, if the truth of the issue does in fact emerge, it is not because of the authority of the one who proposes it but because of the intrinsic coherence of his or her argument.

Many issues that currently are debated with some fervor—she mentioned liturgical styles of worship, church architecture, and private devotions—are not really about faith and morals. Even when the topic is faith and morals, since the time of John Henry Newman it is widely accepted that there is a legitimate development of doctrine in the church. As the traditional faith is passed on from generation to generation, new insights into it may develop.

When it comes, then, to facing issues that are critical to the church in our time, Monika formulates her view in this way: "I see more change, experiment, and conflict as part of the appropriate process of the church defined in the light of the coming Reign of God. I see the prophetic function of the church as People of God in a rapidly changing world. That means a need for discernment and creativity in the contexts which the various segments of the People of God know best."

Deep into the shadowed silences of earth
Love hides the flaming glory
                    Of the royal birth
For which the ages long.
Breaking the air with song
And the heart with yearning.
Just so again this year.
As seeking shelter here,
Love waits.

— from a 1995 Christmas poem
by Monika K. Hellwig

Chapter 3

"Affinity to the Uprooted and the Deprived": Understanding Monika Hellwig's Motherhood

Evelyn Haught

"I thought I'd let you know that soon a young Filipina woman, Letty, will be living with me. She'll have her baby with her."

Monika Hellwig casually spoke these words to my husband Jack[†] and me in 1968, when we were neighbors living in modest rental apartments in Arlington, Virginia. We had already known Monika for almost two years, beginning with our graduate studies at The Catholic University of America in 1966. Jack, like Monika, was in the Religious Studies program and I was in English. During those wonderful days of *aggiornamento*, we met frequently at noon liturgies, especially at Claretian House, where Fr. Gerard Sloyan riveted us with provocative homilies. In September 1967, after Jack and I married, I began teaching at Marymount College (now University) in Arlington, while Jack continued his doctoral studies. After finding our little apartment in Arlington, we were delighted to discover that Monika was living across the street, where she could easily commute to her new teaching position at Georgetown University while writing her dissertation.

We saw each other almost daily and enjoyed frequent casual meals together. Despite the demands of teaching and writing, Monika already exhibited her lifelong gift of hospitality, so it did not seem unusual when she told us that Letty and her baby would be sharing her home. What we did not realize was that this generous gesture signaled her

† Theologian John F. Haught.

fairly rapid movement toward forming a family of her own, through whom she could completely fulfill strong maternal instincts.

Monika had acquired some early experience in mothering. On the eve of World War II, her widowed mother, having already moved the family from Germany to the Netherlands, decided to send her three little girls to Scotland to keep them safe. She instructed Monika to look after her two younger sisters, a task the serious nine-year-old took to heart. Monika's responsibility grew when, shortly after the war, her mother died. Monika was sixteen. The early losses of her family's homes, her parents, her homeland, and other similar pulls on her heart no doubt contributed to a desire to establish a safe haven in her new life in America—and to share it with others who could benefit from a secure environment, such as the young, foreign-born Letty and her illegitimate child. Monika later wrote: "I have always felt a strong affinity to the uprooted and the deprived, probably because I have never been able to see the status quo of any society as normative."[1]

By 1969, Monika had completed her doctorate and moved to a Washington DC high-rise apartment on Tunlaw Road NW, a short walk from Georgetown University. When a position opened, Jack joined Georgetown's theology department and we too found an apartment on Tunlaw Road, again just opposite Monika's building, so our friendship and close familiarity deepened.

In 1970, when I was expecting our first child, Monika told us she had decided to adopt a little girl who was part African-American. She offered no explanation, but, knowing Monika, we didn't expect one. Thus, in September of that year, Erica Hellwig entered all our lives at age eleven months, two months before my baby's birth.

I began babysitting Erica right from the beginning, usually on short notice when something unexpected came up requiring Monika's attention. Erica's most notable feature at that age was a pair of enormous brown eyes that seemed to possess everything around her. Large, loose curls stood pertly atop her head. She was highly energetic, strong-willed, and seemed to make a rapid adjustment to her new mother and life. Monika was enchanted with her and it immediately seemed that she

1. Monika K. Hellwig, "The Mandalas Do Not Break: A Theological Autobiographical Essay," in *Journeys*, ed. Gregory Baum (Mahwah, NJ: Paulist Press, 1975), 128.

had been mothering her entire life. She exuded not only joy but also great self-confidence, something I lacked as a young first-time mom.

Erica reveled in her doting parent's attentions and appeared to blossom under Monika's loving care. Monika, too, flourished, so Jack and I were definitely not surprised when she adopted Michael, aged two and a half, in 1974. Michael, also half African-American, was irresistible, with his dimpled smile and somewhat shy manner. However, with Michael's addition to the Hellwig home jealousy and fear entered Erica's life. Now an adult, Erica admits to feeling threatened by Michael's arrival. She was afraid he would wear her clothes and resented his intrusion into her relationship with her mother.[2] Thus began tension between the Hellwig siblings and maternal challenges that would last the rest of Monika's life.

At this point, Monika sought more space for her growing family and moved to a row house on T Street NW, in the Burleith section of Washington. The house was a few blocks closer to Georgetown University, and the family remained there until 1978. Those were busy years for Monika, who managed to publish with astonishing regularity, achieve academic promotion, give public lectures in addition to her teaching, and nurture two active little children. In the 1970s, when she chose to become a mother, she was unusual. Rare was the full-time working mother; even rarer was the single mother. The added distinction of being a Caucasian woman mothering two black children made her even more unusual in an era when the effects of the Civil Rights Movement still rankled in many Americans. Yet Monika seemed fearless, happy, and fulfilled. So her announcement in 1980 that she was adopting another part African-American child, this time a six-year-old boy named Carlos[3] who had spent most of his life in foster homes, came as just another generous act from this woman whose heart and energy seemed to have no bounds.

Remembering Michael's entrance into their lives, Monika prepared Erica and Michael for the newest member of the family by telling them that it was unfair to Michael to be the sole male in their home, since she and Erica had each other. Therefore, she was adopting Carlos so

2. Erica Hellwig Parker, telephone interview by author, 19 February 2009.
3. This chapter provides limited mention of Carlos Hellwig since he declined permission to be quoted and to have his personal life described at length.

Michael would have a male companion.[4] This seemed acceptable to the two older children, so Carlos's immersion into the family went essentially without incident for them at that moment.

Educating Her Children

Throughout her motherhood, Monika was keenly interested in her children's social, intellectual, physical, and psychological development. So when it was time to send Erica, and then Michael, to school, she chose the Washington Waldorf School, a private nonsectarian school, one of nine hundred worldwide. It states as its mission the cultivation of "each student's capacity to think clearly, feel compassionately, and act purposefully in the world." Its core values are the healthy development of children and adolescents; a balanced, dynamic curriculum; meaningful teacher-student relationships; exceptional teaching; a diverse and inclusive community; a respect for nature; moral discernment; and an active spiritual life.[5] Such values would have been immediately compelling to Monika. But in her desire to provide a meaningful education for Erica and Michael, she miscalculated the impact of two aspects of the school: its emphasis on independent study and the miniscule enrollment of African-American children. When the Hellwig children attended, only two other black children were enrolled. Now an adult, Michael described to me the difficulty they frequently had with learning in an environment that emphasized self-direction and where they felt self-conscious among the many white faces. He said it was the first time he realized he was different and found it initially intimidating.[6] Erica too felt she did not belong, a feeling that would return in most of her subsequent school experiences.[7] In the case of Carlos, Sara Hebeler admiringly described her friend Monika's fierce determination to teach him herself to read and write, something she achieved when he was ten.[8]

4. Erica Hellwig Parker, 19 February 2009.
5. The Washington Waldorf School (accessed 20 February 2009): http://www.washingtonwaldorf.org/AboutUs_091906.html.
6. Michael B. Hellwig, telephone interview by author, 2 February 2009.
7. Erica Hellwig Parker, 19 February 2009.
8. Sara Hebeler, interview by author, McLean, VA, 15 April 2009.

Erica

Monika was devoted to all her children, but from the very beginning, she and Erica developed a unique relationship that evolved into much more than mother-daughter closeness. In all likelihood, gender played a role. Monika had idolized her own birth mother and enjoyed a very loving relationship later on with her "adoptive" mother, Winefride Whale. She was close to her two sisters, Marianne and Angelika, her whole life. Monika also cherished friendships with the Medical Mission Sisters, with whom she had formed lifelong bonds during her fourteen years in the order. So women had been unusually important in her early life. I believe, even when she first adopted Erica, she relished the idea of having this special little female become a crucial part of her life.

When Erica was still very young, Monika, and Erica's godmother, Dr. Andrea Doman, began noticing a tendency toward slouching in the little girl and urged her to stand straight.[9] By age six, Erica began walking strangely. A series of medical examinations and physician visits ensued, which led to increasing frustration but no diagnosis. Finally, a doctor who treated the Washington Redskins professional football team recognized that she needed immediate surgery to correct a severe spinal abnormality. According to the doctor, because of a prenatal defect affecting Erica's lower second and third lumbar vertebrae, which had never joined properly, she was unable to walk correctly and would become paralyzed within two weeks. Monika was stricken by the news but acted with her usual decisiveness and immediately scheduled the surgery at the Children's National Medical Center in Washington DC. During the complicated operation a team of doctors widened the child's spinal canal, rerouted nerves, took a bone fragment from her hip, and fused the vertebrae so she would be able to walk normally. Erica spent eleven months at the hospital in "unbelievable pain." She attributes her ability to endure the ordeal to "my Mom's strength and stoicism—she never surrendered. She saved me from spending the rest of my life in a chair."[10] Monika visited Erica every day of her hospitalization.

9. Michael B. Hellwig, 2 February 2009.
10. Erica Hellwig Parker, 19 February 2009.

Michael Hellwig says he thinks his mother felt profound guilt for the rest of her life for failing to recognize Erica's problem much earlier.[11] Both he and Erica believe Monika had done everything humanly possible and still regret that they could not dissuade her from feeling that she had been negligent. Erica points out that by persevering through so many medical specialists' examinations until she found a diagnosis, Monika demonstrated extraordinary maternal concern and passionate determination to help her child.[12] Nevertheless, this episode and Monika's misgivings about it suggest a possible explanation for her interactions with Erica from this point forward.

Carlos had not yet joined the family during this trying period. Besides having her hands full with Erica's hospitalization, illness, and subsequent physical therapy, Monika was also coping with Michael's serious asthma attacks and bouts of croup. When Erica finally returned to the T Street house, her mother realized that it was not a healthy environment for Michael, and its two-story configuration was not conducive to Erica's rehabilitation and to walking again. In 1978, the family moved to 8408 Galveston Road in Silver Spring, Maryland, where they remained until 1987, living more comfortably on a single level.

The Hellwigs at Home

Moving to Silver Spring ushered in a new era in the life of the Hellwig family. In addition to welcoming Carlos two years after the move to Galveston Road, the older children were developing personal identities, discovering talents, and encountering lifestyles from which they had previously been shielded. Erica displayed genuine artistic ability as well as precocity. I recall many conversations with her when she was a child and preteen, during which she conversed with me as a fellow adult. She was unusually self-possessed and assured. Michael was always polite and a bit reticent, and Carlos was full of fun. Both boys loved sports, especially football, basketball, and track, and exhibited above-average athletic ability—interests outside Monika's experience and somewhat bewildering to her. She marveled at Michael's fearlessness in taking

11. Michael B. Hellwig, 2 February 2009.
12. Erica Hellwig Parker, 19 February 2009.

blows to his body during a football game.[13] During those years our family saw them frequently, particularly at Holy Trinity Catholic Church in Georgetown. Our two boys, who were close in age to Michael and Carlos, used to enjoy playing tag and other games with them on Trinity's school playground. Afterwards, they all made a scramble for the doughnuts, a special treat for the Hellwig children and an incentive to attend church, since Monika was strict about not allowing "junk food" in their home.

The Hellwig children fondly recall the comforts of their home. When they were young, Monika would join them on the floor to play games. She hugged them warmly and delighted in making up pet names for them such as "Erica Luvey," "Noodle Schoondle," and "Michael Rumpelstumple."[14] Michael remembers the joy he always felt upon entering the house after school because Monika made it so welcoming. In winter, a fire always burned. She usually had hot cider warming on the stove, or tea and comfort foods to greet them. He says it was a true haven.[15] All of the children recall that their mother was committed to serving them nutritious meals. She did not allow food to be wasted, telling the children how deprived she and her sisters often were during their childhood as a result of the war. Nevertheless, the children were not above directing a surreptitious morsel or two of disliked dishes to their plump dog Anton, who benefited from their largesse. But they all savored Monika's Saturday and Sunday morning breakfasts. Regular features were eggs, pancakes, and always her delectable homemade crumb cake.[16]

Outside Influences

As they grew older, Monika grew disenchanted with the Waldorf School's ability to meet their unique needs and enrolled them in a succession of other schools, both Catholic and public. The children's academic and social performance became continuing problems. Erica managed to get herself expelled from Regina High School, a Catholic school for girls in Hyattsville, Maryland, for smoking. Michael's grades at the Jesuit Gonzaga College High School in Washington did not measure up to the school's high standards.

13. Sara Hebeler, 15 April 2009.
14. Erica Hellwig Parker, telephone interview by author, 1 April 2009.
15. Michael B. Hellwig, 2 February 2009.
16. Michael B. Hellwig, 2 February 2009.

However, for Erica and Michael, the most significant turning point came with their attending public schools. Some that they attended, because of fixed residential boundaries, were located near the Maryland-District of Columbia border and encompassed several public housing projects. Most of the "project" teenagers there were African-Americans who were much wiser in the ways of the world than the Hellwig children. Both Erica and Michael felt out of their element. Their mother had been diligent in attempting to foster their identities as people of color, even taking them to Africa to understand their racial roots. But up to this point, their interactions with other black people had not encompassed "street-smart" youths whose behavior was raucous at best and criminal at worst. Drug peddling and drug use were commonplace; so was sexual promiscuity. Academic achievement was not a sought-after goal for most of these students. The majority of white students at the school tended to exclude Erica and Michael; the black students found them culturally out of touch and rejected Erica for her light skin color. As self-conscious teenagers, the Hellwig children tried desperately to fit in wherever they could, often with misfits—especially in Erica's case, who was drawn to the "Punks" and "Goths" on the fringes of the student body. They both experimented with drugs. For Michael, this was short-lived. For Erica it proved to be devastating, and she continues to struggle with addiction.[17]

Monika valiantly supported her children's every positive achievement and encouraged any interest they showed that had the potential to uplift them and give them a sense of accomplishment. Nevertheless, when Erica was fifteen, she announced that she had had enough of high school and wanted to drop out to pursue her interest in art. Many parents, especially those with Monika's educational background, might have reacted negatively to such a decision. But Monika encouraged her. This was probably for two reasons: first, Erica was getting nowhere except into deeper trouble, and second, Monika's own mother had abandoned formal schooling at an early age to become an artist:

> My mother was unconventional. . . . She was a cultivated and
> widely knowledgeable person as well as an artist, and it came as a
> great surprise to me when I discovered as a teen-ager that she had

17. Erica Hellwig Parker, 19 February 2009.

demanded to leave school at the age of thirteen. My wise grand-
father allowed it and she never went back, having been thoroughly
disillusioned by what went on in school under the name of education. She went to art school soon after and became totally absorbed
first in drawing and then in sculpture. But she read voraciously
and . . . was constantly in dialog [*sic*] with her father. As an adult,
I was fascinated to learn that Edith Stein . . . had similarly demanded to leave school at the age of thirteen and been permitted
to do so, going on to become a gifted philosopher.[18]

With these two models in mind and at significant financial cost, Monika
supported Erica's enrollment in Washington DC's prestigious Corcoran
College of Art and Design, sponsored by the Corcoran Gallery of Art,
one of America's oldest art museums. Erica passed the challenging
entrance exam with high marks—a testament to her natural talent—
but, lacking the discipline and ambition of Monika's models, attended
the school for only a year. Monika's sister Marianne Hellwig John observed that "[S]he treated her children rationally as she had been treated
by our guardians, without perhaps realising [*sic*] the effect that different
background, expectations and milieu would have on them."[19]

Meanwhile, Erica continued to pursue an irregular path. By this
time, she had become romantically involved with a young man in his
twenties who, unbeknownst to Erica and Monika, was HIV-positive.
From him, Erica herself became HIV-positive and has struggled with
health problems related to AIDS ever since. When Erica was twenty-
three years old, her boyfriend died of a heroin overdose.[20]

The Children's Independent Choices

Monika's professional life, meanwhile, continued to prosper, thanks
to Herculean self-discipline, a deeply imbued sense of responsibility,
great intelligence, and also an ever-growing need to earn enough income
to support the enormous expenses incurred by her children. Few people
outside a small circle of friends and family were aware of the concerns
she experienced in raising her children, especially her unrelenting worry

18. Monika Hellwig, "The Mandalas Do Not Break," 120.
19. Marianne Hellwig John, letter to author, 19 April 2009.
20. Erica Hellwig Parker, 19 February 2009.

over Erica, her health and her future. Thus, she was optimistic when Erica began seeing a young man from Ghana, Julian Parker. Julian seemed stable and mature. Jack and I attended their wedding, a lively tribal event with many guests wearing the colorful native dress of Ghana. Monika appeared happy and hopeful. Alas, the couple separated five years later but never divorced. Tragedy followed. While driving along the New Jersey Turnpike with his brother, Julian entered a rest stop where he was shot to death by an unidentified assailant. The murderer and motive remain unknown. Before he died, Julian was hospitalized for fourteen days in New Jersey. Monika, ever supportive of Erica and concerned about her son-in-law, regularly drove Erica to visit him.[21]

Michael, in the meantime, continued to experience his own ups and downs in school. Determined to help him develop greater discipline, Monika sent him for one year to St. Francis Preparatory School, a Catholic military boarding school in Spring Grove, Pennsylvania. Initially he encountered the familiar problem of being part of a very small racial minority among an essentially white student body, but he made friends and ultimately found this to be a valuable experience. Michael began developing discipline and goals. Upon completing high school, he decided to enter the U.S. Marine Corps, in which he served honorably for four years. He subsequently established a security firm that provides services to foreign embassies and diplomatic personnel. Monika was very proud of what he made of himself. Today he is an exceptionally handsome man with a keen sense of responsibility, who appears to model his behavior after his mother's. He frequently mentions with admiration Monika's "consistently optimistic outlook on life, even when everything around her seemed to be crumbling. She was always calm and would always tell us, 'We can get through this.'"[22]

Indeed, Monika somehow always did, and it is not overstating her life as a mother to say that her faith sustained her. By 1987, Monika was living at 2219 Laurel Hill Way in Germantown, Maryland, overlooking a lake. Several years later she moved yet again to another Maryland suburb, Gaithersburg, where she took an apartment at 716 Clopper Road. In the spring of 1994, she registered as a parishioner at St. Rose of Lima Catholic Church, where she remained active until her death.

21. Ibid.
22. Michael B. Hellwig, 2 February 2009.

The parish became a great source of strength to her, but her faith in general was an ever-sustaining and central force in her life. No matter how difficult her life became, she made time each day for prayer and contemplation. Michael Hellwig says he cannot recall a single day when she failed to rise early, usually about five o'clock in the morning, to read Scripture and then pray alone in her room. The children, despite whatever else was happening in their lives, respected this special time she reserved for contemplation and refrained from interrupting her.[23]

Monika: A Devoted Mother, a Generous Heart

Monika viewed her role of mother as seriously as she did her professional roles and tried with great dedication to raise her children in an orderly, disciplined home conducive to learning and to loving one another. When the children were young she refused to allow a television in the house so they would not be distracted from their studies. Michael Hellwig, describing how desperately he and Carlos wanted to watch the 1982 NCAA national championship basketball game between Georgetown University and the University of North Carolina, told me how the boys begged their mother to allow the family to borrow a TV for the occasion, to which she agreed.[24] From the beginning, she enjoyed reading to her children, especially British childhood classics such as *The Chronicles of Narnia* and *The Wind in the Willows*.[25] She required them to help with household chores and maintained strict standards. Michael recalls with humor that dusting "properly" required almost military precision.[26]

Could Monika have done anything differently in raising her children? As I alluded to earlier, from the very beginning of her motherhood she appears to have displayed an unusual relationship with her daughter. This relationship, as the years went by, seemed to prevent her from exercising the "tough love" that every parent at some point must, no matter how distasteful. Most of Monika's intimates were keenly aware of this tendency toward leniency with Erica and frequently expressed

---

23. Ibid.
24. Michael B. Hellwig, interview with author, 13 May 2009.
25. Erica Hellwig Parker, telephone interview by author, 12 March 2009.
26. Michael B. Hellwig, 13 May 2009.

concern for both mother and daughter. Her sister Marianne, the mother of six, has observed: "My children had to learn early that I was a fallible human being, with likes, dislikes, moods and needs. I don't think Monika found it easy to draw boundaries to give herself the time, space and silence that she needed, especially in regard to her daughter. . . . I begged [Monika] to follow professional advice on 'tough love' for both her daughter's and her own good, but this she was unable to do. She traveled hopefully despite the experience of constant let down."[27]

Problematic though her relationship with Erica may have been, I find it impossible to fault Monika. In every way, she lived primarily to make these children feel loved and protected. Perhaps she should have drawn firmer boundaries for her daughter, but I believe she saw in Erica some fragile void that she felt only her unrelenting love and unconditional acceptance could fill. As a parent myself, I can easily tally up hundreds of instances where I might have acted more judiciously. But can a parent who sacrificed as much as Monika did be faulted for loving too much? Her friend from St. Rose of Lima parish, Sue Clark, provides an insightful summation of Monika's motherhood: "Monika lived in the PRESENT. She exemplified how not to get stuck with what happened in the past (the kids' pre-natal, infancy . . .) or with the mistakes that the kids made last year or last week. If there was something to be addressed at the moment, she addressed it, with incredible forgiveness and magnanimity. She did not see their actions as a reflection on her so she didn't waste time (or energy) feeling sorry for herself, denying the error of their ways or making the issue about herself."[28]

Monika lived a life of great generosity to others and remarkable selflessness, characteristics that must be taken into account when reflecting on her relationship with Erica. Her son Michael describes an incident that occurred when he was quite young but one that was clearly a significant teaching moment for him. On a very cold winter day in downtown Washington, the family was waiting in a long line outside a theater to attend a play. Suddenly an obviously homeless man approached the line. Everyone in the line quickly moved away to avoid any contact with him, but Monika held the children firmly and did not move. The man approached her and asked for a handout. She quickly opened her

27. Marianne Hellwig John, letter, 19 April 2009.
28. Suzanne C. Clark, e-mail communication to author, 27 May 2009.

wallet and gave him its entire contents, about sixty dollars. The children asked her why she gave him so much money, and she replied that he needed it. When they protested that he might be lying, she responded that he still probably needed some help, so she lost nothing through the transaction. Michael says she was like that with everyone. She looked at all people equally. "She provided us with many learning opportunities through her own example,"[29] he told me appreciatively.

Following Monika's death, her friend Karen Maury entered the last house where Monika lived, 9211 Mintwood Street in Silver Spring, Maryland, in preparation for its sale. Monika had moved there in 1998. Karen noted that Monika's bedroom was the smallest in the house and was furnished in spartan manner, with simply a twin bed, other basic furnishings, and no adornments.[30] Monika had given Erica the much larger master bedroom when Erica moved back home after her separation from Julian. Michael Hellwig says this typified his mother, whom he described as the least materialistic person he has ever known. The children knew that, years before, she had decided to remain faithful to the vows she had taken when she had been a religious. Michael says he never knew her to depart from them.[31]

As for her children's religious education, Monika took them to church when they were young but did not require church attendance as they grew older. Rather, she encouraged them to be thoughtful about their religious lives and make personal choices that were meaningful to them. As young children, they attended Catholic Confraternity of Christian Doctrine (CCD) classes at Holy Trinity Church, and the family prayed together. She helped them observe religious holy days and made a ritual of such activities as lighting the Advent wreath in the home. They expressed thanks before their meals.[32] But she never adopted a dogmatic approach to their religious education, which, to Jack and me, was in keeping with her overall theological orientation.

29. Michael B. Hellwig, 13 May 2009.
30. Karen Maury, interview by author, Silver Spring, Maryland, 14 April 2009.
31. Michael B. Hellwig, 13 May 2009.
32. Michael B. Hellwig, 13 May 2009; Erica Hellwig Parker, 12 March 2009.

Why Did Monika Adopt?

Why did Monika Hellwig adopt these children? She herself does not appear ever to have articulated a reason, but I believe it is one of the most compelling aspects of her life. Both of Monika's sisters believe that their own early lives may have influenced her to adopt: "The example of our dear guardians [Winefride and Barrett Whale] will certainly have played a part in Monika's decision to adopt, though from very early on she had a great sense of responsibility for others," Marianne Hellwig John has stated.[33] Angelika Hellwig Collis echoes this belief: "Monika may have thought that we owed it to humanity to plough back into the world the luck and love that we ourselves had found."[34]

I put this question to a number of her friends, colleagues, and relatives, and it was interesting that everyone answered it in essentially the same way: it was what Jesus Christ called her to do. Monika's commitment to "living the word" cannot be overstated. It was the driving force of her entire life, and I have never known anyone who lived it more faithfully.

In her 1985 Madeleva Lecture in Spirituality, Monika provided several insights into how she believed the Christian's life should be led: "[W]hat are the needs of the community and what is the capacity of this individual or group to respond to those needs? Where the two intersect, the call of God is to be found. But this implies that a vocation is not a call issued once in a lifetime, leaving the rest blueprinted and dispensing of the need for further discernment. Rather it suggests that vocational choices are being made and must be made continuously throughout one's life."[35] In the case of her own life, she made a vocational choice to be a mother, despite the many complications this role would introduce to a life that was already satisfying, interesting, and full of promise. She *freely chose to be encumbered* by them.

In 1984, she provided a slight glimpse into the challenges she was experiencing as a single parent when she wrote: "The most obvious and most urgent need of the Christian single parent is for a deep life of prayer because of the loneliness of the situation. For most women and

33. Marianne Hellwig John, letter, 19 April 2009.

34. Angelika Hellwig Collis, letter to author, 22 February 2009.

35. Monika K. Hellwig, *Christian Women in A Troubled World* (Mahwah, NJ: Paulist Press, 1985), 31–32.

men constant interaction with children has its satisfactions but is on the whole severely draining."[36] She did not attempt to disguise the difficulty of her life as a parent:

> Unless [single parents] are very fortunate in having extended family nearby, they are, so to speak, never "off duty," and are drained to exhaustion by constant demands for attention, sympathy, enthusiasm, a listening ear, personal services of all kinds, transportation, school meetings, doctors, dentists, clothes, food shopping, and so on, usually with the youngest children always tagging along and becoming fretful, demanding, disruptive, while everyone turns accusing eyes on the parent who cannot cope with the situation and has broken the unspoken rules by bringing small children along.[37]

Monika described the life of the single parent as a "treadmill existence"[38] when she wrote that single parents "come home from a full days [sic] work to begin the night shift at home, day after day, night after night. Most do not get enough sleep—ever. Most do not get the minimum of private time that we all need—ever."[39]

Perhaps Monika was unable to impose stricter discipline on the children because of the crushing fatigue that grew constantly worse through all the years I knew her:

> It is the complete and permanent exhaustion that makes it so difficult, because the parent is often in the same position as a prisoner who is being brainwashed. The fatigue and consequent depression are indescribable to anyone not constantly subjected to it. Paradoxically, it is this terrible state of inescapable fatigue that makes it almost impossible for the working single parent to resist the demands either of the children or of outside forces because it takes a certain degree of self-possession and personal focus to say no. The greatest temptation of the single parent is to give up and let the children do what they want, whether or not it is good for them or for others, reasonable in itself, or manageable for the parent.[40]

36. Monika K. Hellwig, "Christian Spirituality for the Single Parent," *Spirituality Today* 36, no. 1 (Spring 1984): 47.
37. Ibid.
38. Ibid, 48.
39. Ibid.
40. Ibid.

Monika's colleague and former vice president of the Association of Catholic Colleges and Universities, Michael James, said: "She gave her life to her children. It wasn't about seeking fulfillment for her. It was . . . of being nothing for the other person. She surrendered all her professional competencies and control to love [her children] unconditionally. She viewed her motherhood as a gift."[41] I agree with his observation that most of us who knew her well and saw her often never perceived in her any sense that her motherhood was a burden, despite the fact that it physically exhausted her.

Monika wrote that the ultimate Christian demand "is that of charity, of love of God which is expressed most unambiguously in loving care for the most needy, justice for the most oppressed, and peace in human society."[42] In Erica, Michael, and Carlos, she saw three among the most needy—racially mixed children, whose complexions and other physical features would mark them as undesirable to most Americans who were willing to adopt children in the latter part of the twentieth century. Carlos had the added disadvantage of being well beyond a standard adoption age, as he himself noted at the time of her death: "Even though I didn't know it at that time, I was approaching an age where it would become increasingly more difficult for me to be adopted. In institutional terms, I was about to become a 'hopeless cause.' My Mom's love and support changed all that. My mom [*sic*] took the chance and with hope for my future made that sacrifice."[43]

Sue Clark describes Monika as having "had such a big sense of the Church and such an expansive view of what Jesus called us to do." In regard to why Monika adopted, Sue believes that she "did what was in her hands to do, following Jesus' call."[44] I think this explains why Monika adopted. She herself, in writing about the attributes we know of Jesus as described in scriptural portraits and "the memory of the Church community to this day," identified, as perhaps the most important, compassion. "Compassion means more than feeling sorrow over the

41. Michael J. James, telephone interview by author, 6 March 2009.

42. Hellwig, *Christian Women*, 35.

43. Carlos Hellwig, "Family Reflections," quoted in the eulogy delivered by Michael J. James, Mass of Christian Burial for Monika K. Hellwig, St. Rose of Lima Catholic Church, Gaithersburg, Maryland, 6 October 2005.

44. Suzanne C. Clark, telephone interview by author, 17 April 2009.

suffering of another. It means entering deeply into the experience of the other."[45]

That Monika did, first with her sisters, later with Letty and her baby and so many others, and most of all with her children. I believe that becoming their mother gave her the greatest satisfactions and joys of her life, "the feeling that she had given a good Christian home to three children who might otherwise have lived their childhood years in institutions and later not have had much chance in life. Making up to them for being abandoned."[46]

Monika's Legacy as a Mother

What is Monika Hellwig's legacy as a mother? The answer is found in the free and generous expressions of love for her by her children. "She was the best mother in the world,"[47] Erica told me with great feeling. Michael, a budding poet, perhaps provides the most poignant answer: "She saved our lives twice: first, through adopting us, and second, through her death, which has gradually been helping the three of us develop adult relationships with one another. We're finally beginning to listen to one another and to accept each other for who and what each of us is. We're finally learning to respect one another."[48]

Sources

Clark, Suzanne C. E-mail communication to author. 27 May 2009.

———. Telephone interview by author. 17 April 2009.

Collis, Angelika Hellwig. Letter to author. 22 February 2009.

Haughey, John C. Homily. Memorial Mass for Monika K. Hellwig. Holy Trinity Catholic Church, Washington, DC, 8 October 2005.

Haught, John F. Conversations with author. Falls Church, Virginia, January–May 2009.

Hebeler, John and Sara. Interview by author. McLean, Virginia, 15 April 2009.

---

45. Hellwig, *Christian Women*, 40.
46. Angelika Hellwig Collis, letter, 22 February 2009.
47. Erica Hellwig Parker, 19 February 2009.
48. Michael B. Hellwig, 2 February 2009.

Hellwig, Michael B. Interview by author. Falls Church, Virginia, 13 May 2009.

————. Telephone interview with author. 2 February 2009.

Hellwig, Monika K. *A Catholic Scholar's Journey through the Twentieth Century*. Dayton, OH: The University of Dayton, 1993.

————. "Christian Spirituality for the Single Parent." *Spirituality Today* 36, no. 1 (Spring 1984): 47–55.

————. *Christian Women in a Troubled World*. Mahwah, NJ: Paulist Press, 1985.

————. "The Mandalas Do Not Break: A Theological Autobiographical Essay." In *Journeys*, edited by Gregory Baum. Mahwah, NJ: Paulist Press, 1975.

James, Michael J. Eulogy. Mass of Christian Burial for Monika K. Hellwig. St. Rose of Lima Catholic Church, Gaithersburg, Maryland, 6 October 2005.

————. Telephone interview by author. 6 March 2009.

John, Marianne Hellwig. Correspondence with author. 19 April 2009.

————. Telephone conversation with author. 20 March 2009.

John, Simon. Telephone interview by author. 22 March 2009.

Maury, Karen. Interview by author. Silver Spring, Maryland, 14 April 2009.

Parker, Erica Hellwig. Telephone interviews by author. 19 February, 2 March, 12 March, and 1 April 2009.

Piness, Nancy J. Telephone conversation with author. 3 March 2009.

Tambasco, Anthony J. Conversation with author. Falls Church, Virginia, 16 April 2009.

The Washington Waldorf School (accessed 20 February 2009): http://www .washingtonwaldorf.org/AboutUs_091906.html.

When I reflect on what theology is for me now, I realize that first of all it is not a career I have chosen but a task that somehow landed in front of me to be done. Secondly, it is a task that is done primarily from the resources of my own life experience within a great tradition that I am very happy to have internalized, for which I have the deepest affection and respect, and for which I consider myself co-responsible. Beyond that it is a task in which intellectual endeavors are only the tip of the iceberg that shows. The reason I engage in it is mainly that it gives me great satisfaction and that it seems to meet a need as basic as those I set out to meet in Liverpool and had hoped to meet in India.

— from "The Mandalas Do Not Break:
A Theological Autobiographical Essay"
by Monika K. Hellwig

Chapter 4

Welcomed to Wisdom's Feast: Memories of Monika as Professor and Mentor

Rosemary P. Carbine

Does not Wisdom call, and does not understanding raise
   her voice?
   On the heights, beside the way, at the crossroads she takes
her stand;
Beside the gates in the front of the town, at the entrance of
   the portals she cries out:
"To you, O people, I call, and my cry is to all that live.
O simple ones, learn prudence; acquire intelligence, you who
   lack it.
Hear, for I will speak noble things, and from my lips will come
   what is right."

Wisdom has built her house; she has hewn her seven pillars.
She has slaughtered her animals, she has mixed her wine,
   she has also set her table.
She has sent out her servant girls, she calls from the highest
   places in the town:
"You that are simple, turn in here!" To those without sense,
   she says,
"Come, eat of my bread and drink of the wine that I have mixed.
Lay aside immaturity, and live, and walk in the way of insight."

Proverbs 8:1-6; 9:1-6

I encountered Monika Hellwig near the end of my college career
and near the end of her more than three decades of teaching in the

department of theology at Georgetown University. During my senior year on the Hilltop, I enrolled in her famed two-course sequence in the History of Christian Thought, spanning fall 1993 and spring 1994. I anticipated two semesters of seeing the cumulative history of Christian beliefs, texts, peoples, and practices through the eyes and lived experiences of one of its own contemporary makers. Monika served as a ghostwriter and research assistant for a Vatican official at the Second Vatican Council (1962–1965), as president of the Catholic Theological Society of America in 1986 when Charles E. Curran dissented from noninfallible church teachings on sexual ethics and consequently lost his theological license to teach in Catholic universities, and as Landegger Distinguished Professor of Theology for six years at Georgetown. My classmates and I were not disappointed.

One of those classmates, Rev. Julie Ann Armstrong Perks, is an ordained Anglican priest who recently took the not-so-conservative name Magdalena when she joined a plain-dressing Anglican order with roots in the Mennonites and Conservative Quakers. Julian, or Julianne, as she was known to her college classmates and professors, shared with me some memories about Monika's teaching and its impact on her own theology and vocation. Julian recalled in a personal e-mail that "she once told me that I had a better grasp of the nature of eternity than St. Augustine. I am still not sure if that was an ironic remark, but I treasure it. I also used my notes from History of Christian Thought many times as I preached and taught confirmation classes. It was an important, seminal course for me as a priest."

Fifteen years after taking those two courses, my strongest memory involves Monika sitting at a desk in the front of the class with open books, notes, and hands, engaging the texts and students' interpretations of the texts—in other words, calling us to immerse ourselves *in* as well as make our own marks *on* the history of the Christian tradition. Monika's courses required such extensive time commitments and independent theological thinking that I would warn potential students (or so I am reminded by former classmates, though I don't recall doing so) to drop the course unless majoring in the subject. Consulting the syllabi, notes, and papers from those courses reveals Monika's high standards and requirements for undergraduate students: weekly readings of primary and secondary sources (e.g., Cyril Richardson, Justo Gonzalez, and William Placher), active class discussions of those readings, two independent presentations on selected readings of the students' choice, and intensive writing assignments—in the first course, a ten- to fifteen-page midterm and final paper, and in the second course, six four- to six-page critical reflection papers! Monika's teaching as illustrated in this small sample of her courses certainly shaped students to become informed, intelligent laity.[1] She built on that long teaching history when she later commented as executive director of the Association of Catholic Colleges and Universities that "the question is whether the task of higher education in our pluralistic changing society is to lock students into rules—even rules I agree with—or to teach them critical thinking."[2] She personally—along with Langdon Gilkey, Chester Gillis, Jack Haught, Diana Hayes, Julia Lamm, Alan Mitchell, and other Georgetown professors between 1990 and 1994— inspired me to pursue graduate studies in theology at the University of Chicago Divinity School.

From the perspectives of feminist theology and theological education (two areas of my theological training), I look back through the lens of the Wisdom tradition to interpret my main memory of Monika as a professor and mentor. Feminist theologians and biblical scholars have critically appropriated the Wisdom tradition to challenge masculinist language for God and patriarchal restrictions on the imitation as well as sacramental signification of Christ.[3] From a feminist perspective, the Wisdom tradition found in the biblical and apocryphal texts of Proverbs, Sirach, the Wisdom of Solomon, and others describes a female personification of the divine who participates in creating, redeeming,

---

1. Monika Hellwig wrote extensively on the vocation of teaching; see "The Catholic Intellectual Tradition in the Catholic University" and "Teaching as Vocation," in *Examining the Catholic Intellectual Tradition*, 2 vols., ed. Anthony J. Cernera and Oliver J. Morgan (Fairfield, CT: Sacred Heart University Press, 2002).

2. Quoted in Tamar Levin, "Catholics Adopt More Liberal Attitudes During Their Years in College, A Survey Finds," *New York Times*, March 5, 2003: B8.

3. Elizabeth Johnson, *She Who Is: Mystery of God in Feminist Theological Discourse* (New York: Crossroad, 1992); idem, "Redeeming the Name of Christ: Christology," in *Freeing Theology: The Essentials of Theology in Feminist Perspective*, ed. Catherine Mowry LaCugna (New York: HarperCollins, 1993), 115–37; Elisabeth Schüssler Fiorenza, *In Memory of Her: A Feminist Theological Reconstruction of Christian Origins* (New York: Crossroad, 1983); and, idem, *Jesus: Miriam's Child, Sophia's Prophet* (New York: Continuum, 1994).

and sustaining everyday life, especially by acting as prophetic street preacher and banquet host of justice and peace. Within the vast literature on theological education, or the teaching and learning of theology and religious studies in undergraduate and graduate programs, educators like Peter C. Hodgson reclaim and retrieve the Wisdom tradition for its pedagogical potential to rethink *paideia*, or education for critical thinking and character formation.[4] Reflecting on the portrait of Wisdom in the Wisdom of Solomon 7:22–8:1, Hodgson observes that "Sophia defines the kind of Spirit that God's Spirit is—not a possessing, displacing, controlling Spirit but a persuading, inviting, educing, communicating, teaching Spirit, acting in profound interaction with human spirit, indeed the whole cosmos."[5]

When viewed against the backdrop of these theological perspectives on Wisdom, Monika incarnated Wisdom in both the context and content of her teaching. Recalling the second set of verses from Proverbs that opened this essay, Monika welcomed students with open hands and books to Wisdom's feast, housing and nourishing us on the beliefs, practices, and texts of Christians across diverse and divergent times and cultures. In addition, she invited, not coerced, college students (as well as colleagues and parishioners) to practice theology, or to "lay aside immaturity, and live" in Christianity as a dynamic tradition that is transmitted and (re)invented throughout its history by ordinary and extraordinary folk alike, whether or not they belonged to the Christian faith.[6] From this viewpoint, Monika's teaching for faith-based critical,

---

4. Peter C. Hodgson, *God's Wisdom: Toward a Theology of Education* (Louisville, KY: Westminster John Knox Press, 1999). Hodgson builds on Edward Farley and David Kelsey, who previously constructed theologies of education that bridged a longstanding divide between *Wissenschaft* or the critical study of disciplines (including theology) in universities, and *paideia*, or the cultivation of personal virtues or habits of mind and heart through that study. See Edward Farley, *Theologia: The Fragmentation and Unity of Theological Education* (Philadelphia: Fortress Press, 1983), chaps. 6–7; and David Kelsey, *Between Athens and Berlin: The Theological Education Debate* (Grand Rapids, MI: Eerdmans, 1993), chaps. 1, 6.

5. Hodgson, *God's Wisdom*, 93.

6. Hellwig described the transmission of traditions, Catholic and otherwise, as a main goal of Catholic institutions of higher education. See "Theological Education in the Undergraduate Core Curriculum," in *Theological Education in the Catholic Tradition: Contemporary Challenges*, ed. Patrick W. Carey and Earl C. Muller (New York: Crossroad, 1997), 68–79, esp. 70, 75.

imaginative, and transformative thinking and living had an emancipatory effect, as described by Hodgson: "to draw people out of their daily preoccupations and petty provincialisms into an encounter with the eternal, with ultimate truth and value, with unbounded love, with a radical transformative freedom"[7]—especially into an encounter with what constituted the liberating Christian tradition.

Idealizing Monika as a contemporary personification of Woman Wisdom may fall prey to romanticizing official church ideals of Catholic women as self-giving to the point of self-sacrificing vowed religious, wives, and mothers.[8] Indeed, Proverbs is bookended by parallel portraits of Wisdom (Prov 1–9) and the capable wife (Prov 31). Both figures are characterized as full of trust, goodness, strength, charity, dignity, wisdom, kindness, honor, and fear of the Lord. Both figures are also contrasted with the alien or strange woman, who is described as a smooth-talking and seductive, wayward and wily, loud, sexually independent, and religiously impure woman (Prov 2:16-19; 5:3-6; 7:5-27). Biblical scholar Claudia Camp cautions against the patriarchal implications of the Wisdom tradition, which replicate and reinscribe longstanding stereotypes of the virtues and vices of good and bad sorts of women.[9] However, Monika trumped or outright transgressed persistent gender and hierarchical dualisms. She continually resisted binary (i.e., either/or) thinking about gender and religious identity, creating opportunities outside the classroom for teaching about liberating Christianity by her own example.

In her personal life, she combined academic achievement and leadership with single motherhood, leaving a lasting impression on stu-

---

7. Hodgson, *God's Wisdom*, 98, cf. 110.

8. For a critical theological and political response to recent papal writings on the ontological maternal nature of women, see Rosemary P. Carbine, "'Artisans of a New Humanity': Revisioning the Public Church in a Feminist Perspective," in *Frontiers in Catholic Feminist Theology: Shoulder to Shoulder*, ed. Susan Abraham and Elena Procario-Foley (Minneapolis: Fortress, 2009). By contrast, so-called authentic or true Catholic feminists aim to actualize such official church teachings on the maternal "genius" of women; for a theological interpretation of this "feminist" movement, see Tina Beattie, *New Catholic Feminism: Theology and Theory* (New York: Routledge, 2006).

9. See Claudia Camp, *Wisdom and the Feminine in the Book of Proverbs* (Decatur, GA: Almond Press, 1985); and idem, *Wise, Strange, and Holy: The Strange Woman and the Making of the Bible* (Sheffield: Sheffield Academic Press, 2000).

dents. Another former classmate, Zachary Dziedzic, graduated from Georgetown in 1994 and received his MA from Fordham University. Zach currently teaches history at Loyola Blakefield, a Jesuit men's high school in Towson, Maryland. Zach regretted that he never had Monika in class because his double major in government and theology/religious studies often offered conflicting courses. He recalled, however, that he "always admired her work, but even more I was impressed by her personal story. My sister is adopted, and I was profoundly impressed by her [Monika's] commitment to her three adopted children."

In her scholarly life, she addressed the topic of virtues in religion and politics in one of her last books, which reconciled some of the most commonly construed at-odds virtues of conformity and dissent, obedience and conscience, humility and power, loyalty to tradition and openness to change in both religious and political life, among others.[10] She embodied and epitomized those virtues for fellow theologians in her continuing career after Georgetown in educational administration. Like Wisdom personified in the first set of verses from Proverbs as a prophetic woman street preacher standing at the gates, heights, and crossroads of the town, Monika advocated in a rather outspoken way for the combination of Catholic identity and the Catholic intellectual tradition as president of the Association of Catholic Colleges and Universities between 1996 and 2005.

Monika's tenure as the ACCU president coincided with major moments in Catholic higher education that also impacted my own theological career. I completed my masters and doctoral studies in theology at the University of Chicago Divinity School (1994–2001) around the same time that the American Catholic bishops, leading figures in Catholic higher education like Monika, and the Vatican negotiated specific norms for localizing *Ex Corde Ecclesiae* in the United States, an instruction issued in 1990 on sustaining Catholic identity within Catholic higher

10. Hellwig, *Public Dimensions of a Believer's Life: Rediscovering the Cardinal Virtues* (Lanham, MD: Rowman & Littlefield, 2005). Hellwig stands in good company with Catholic and non-Catholic theological and ethical reflection on formation for responsible citizenship in U.S. public life, by, for example, Francis Schüssler Fiorenza, Ronald Thiemann, and Jeffrey Stout. For a feminist theological approach to virtuous citizenry articulated in response to these public/political theologians, see Carbine, "Ekklesial Work: Toward a Feminist Public Theology," *Harvard Theological Review* 99, no. 4 (October 2006): 433–55.

education.[11] Moreover, Monika retired from the presidency of the ACCU in 2005, during my junior sabbatical leave from College of the Holy Cross, at a time when the U.S. Catholic bishops prioritized dealing with the aftermath of the clergy sexual abuse crisis in the United States. The bishops attended to the clergy sex abuse crisis rather than sift through faculty applications from their diocese's colleges for the mandatum or a license to teach Catholic theology, ethics, Scripture, history, and so on as indicated by the Vatican's 1990 decree *Ex Corde Ecclesiae*—or so many Catholic theologians thought.[12] Monika's legacy as a messenger of Wisdom—as a formidable advocate for the Catholic intellectual tradition and for the academic freedom of Catholic scholars within that tradition in the aftermath of *Ex Corde*—has propelled me to reflect further on recent events in Catholic higher education regarding the religious identity or "brand" of Catholic colleges and the academic freedom of Catholic theologians.[13]

In U.S. corporate and popular culture, a "brand statement" popularizes and sells a company's, institution's, or person's identity. Different brands relative to religion and gender dominated U.S. politics in the fast-paced weeks prior to the 2008 U.S. presidential election. Democratic presidential nominee Sen. Barack Obama was persistently regarded as Muslim, a religious label that rendered him an unfit candidate for a ma(i)nly WASP-ish White House. Muslim was wielded to "other," to sustain both Christian political supremacy as well as American exceptionalism. Muslim also served as religious secret code for expressing racist views in a post-9/11 United States. Republican vice-presidential

11. Mary Theresa Moser, RSCJ, outlines some of the theological, canonical, and other institutional precedents for *Ex Corde Ecclesiae* in "Between A Rock and a Hard Place: Theologians and the Mandatum," *Horizons* 27, no. 2 (Fall 2000): 322–37.

12. Beth McMurtrie, "Silence, Not Confrontation over the Mandatum," *The Chronicle of Higher Education* 48, no. 40 (June 14, 2002): A10–A11. Indeed, Hellwig, along with nearly forty Catholic business leaders, academics, and prominent laity in media and other fields, attended a daylong conference with some U.S. Catholic bishops to discuss the future of the U.S. church in the aftermath of the clergy sex abuse scandal. See Michael Paulson, "Bishops Seek Out Opinions, In Private Conference Focus is Church Future," *Boston Globe*, July 11, 2003: A1.

13. The following pages build on my conference paper for a panel titled "The Politics of Naming and Branding in the Academy, Publishing, and Public Policy," sponsored by the Feminist Liberation Theologians Network meeting at the annual meeting of the American Academy of Religion on October 31, 2008.

nominee Gov. Sarah Palin was draped with the mantle of feminism, a gender politics that allegedly appealed to disaffected supporters of Sen. Hillary Clinton's Democratic presidential bid. The feminist label signified Palin as palatable to women due to a biologically-deterministic type of representational identity politics, i.e., any woman regardless of political platform represents women and feminism. It also made Palin acceptable to elite "Wall Street" as well as everyday "Main Street" men. That is to say, Palin's nonthreatening "add women and stir" approach to politics empowered women to sit at the current political table without altering its architecture of pro-corporate, pro-conservative sexual ethics, pro-military seats, and thereby excluding other feminist agendas for social justice and peace.

Based on these few examples, the brands of religion and gender marketed in recent U.S. politics served to articulate a discourse and practice of "othering" that spurred demonization and exclusion of those labeled "other." So too with the politics of branding feminist theology and studies in religion within the Catholic academy. The following paragraphs examine the intersections of feminist theology and studies in religion with educational politics on Catholic campuses, especially regarding their different perspectives on academic freedom and their implications to shape students for participation in U.S. as well as broader global public life.

Reflecting a rising consumerist approach to the commodification of education, Catholic higher education has utilized the "brand statement" to distinguish and market its signature contributions to liberal arts and professional schools.[14] In doing so, Catholic higher education finds itself at odds with feminist theology and studies in religion about academic freedom. While most U.S. Catholic colleges, universities, and academic guilds endorsed the American Association of Colleges and the American Association of University Professors policies in the late 1960s,[15] issues about academic freedom in Catholic higher education resurfaced recently through two major events, namely, the papal visit

14. For example, see "Marketing and Mission," *Conversations on Jesuit Higher Education* 25 (2004): 3–37.

15. For a history of academic freedom within U.S. Catholic higher education, see Charles E. Curran, *Catholic Higher Education, Theology, and Academic Freedom* (Notre Dame, IN: University of Notre Dame Press, 1990).

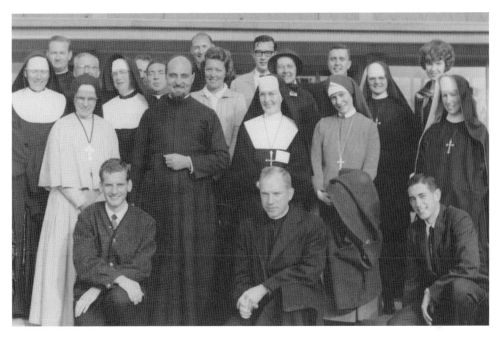

Monika as Sr. Mary Cuthbert at a retreat at Rocca di Papa outside Rome sponsored by the Movement for a Better World. She is in the second row, second from the right.

Monika K. Hellwig.

Monika with her first adopted child, daughter Erica. Christmas 1970.

Forum held February 1994 to inaugurate the celebration of Woodstock
Theological Center's 20th year. Left to right: Avery Dulles, SJ, Monika K. Hellwig,
and E.J. Dionne.

Participants in The
Woodstock Forum
held May 2, 1995:
seated, left to right,
Kenneth L.
Woodward and
Monika K. Hellwig;
standing left to right,
Kenneth R. Himes,
OFM, and Most Rev.
James W. Malone.

Madeleva Lecturers, Convergence 2000, held April 30, 2000, at Saint Mary's College, Notre Dame, Indiana. Front row, left to right: Mary Catherine Hilkert, OP, Diana L. Hayes, Sandra M. Schneiders, IHM, Monika K. Hellwig, Marilou Eldred, President, Margaret Brennan, IHM; back row, left to right: Joan Chittister, OSB, Lisa Sowle Cahill, Elizabeth Johnson, CSJ, Denise Lardner Carmody, Mary C. Boys, SNJM, Elizabeth Dreyer, Gail Mandell, Dolores R. Leckey, Maria Harris, Kathleen Norris, Jeanette Rodriquez, Rose Ann Schultz, CSC, Vice President. (R. E. Koehler Photographics Studio)

Left to right: Joan Chittister, OSB, Monika K. Hellwig, Diana L. Hayes, Convergence 2000. (R. E. Koehler Photographics Studio)

Monika K. Hellwig at the Convergence 2000 gathering of the Madeleva Lecturers, April 2000. (R. E. Koehler Photographics Studio)

A Monika Hellwig Symposium held at Saint Mary's College, Notre Dame, Indiana, October 8–9, 2009. A working session for authors and editors to discuss their particular contributions to the book and their insights concerning Monika Hellwig's impact on the church in our time. The gathering included a public session.

to the United States in April 2008 and the nonappointment of Rosemary Radford Ruether at the University of San Diego in July 2008. These events illustrate two different perspectives on academic freedom supported respectively by the institutional Catholic Church and by Catholic feminist scholars in theology and religious studies.

During his U.S. visit in April 2008, Pope Benedict XVI delivered a speech to Catholic educators at The Catholic University of America that held important implications for the religious identity and academic freedom of Catholic colleges and universities.[16] In his speech, the current pope stated that "any appeal to the principle of academic freedom in order to justify positions that contradict the faith and the teaching of the church would obstruct or even betray the university's identity and mission." Pope Benedict reinforced the *Application of* Ex Corde Ecclesiae *for the United States*, effective in 2001,[17] which states that theologians participate in the teaching mission of the local bishop and church (Appl. I, par. 3; cf. Appl. II, Art. 4, par. 4) and thus must enjoy "full communion" with the church in their research and teaching. Although theologians dispute the meaning of "full communion,"[18] the institutional church defines it in juridical terms: to "present authentic Catholic teaching" and "to be faithful to the church's magisterium" relative to its interpretation of Scripture, tradition, doctrine, and morals (Appl. II, Art. 4, par. 4). Indeed, Robert Egan has observed: "If I teach in virtue of my baptism and my own academic and professional competence, and if there is no question here of 'an appointment, authorization, delegation,

---

16. Pope Benedict XVI, "Meeting with Catholic Educators: Address of His Holiness Benedict XVI (Rome: Libreria Editrice Vaticana, April 17, 2008), available at http:// www.vatican.va/ holy_father/benedict_xvi/speeches/2008/april/documents/hf_ben -xvi_spe_20080417_cath-univ-washington_en.html.

17. United States Conference of Catholic Bishops, *Application of* Ex Corde Ecclesiae *for the United States*, June 1, 2000, and reprinted in Committee on Education of the United States Conference of Catholic Bishops, *Catholic Identity in Our Colleges and Universities: A Collection of Defining Documents* (Washington, DC: USCCB, 2006).

18. Dennis M. Doyle, "Communion Ecclesiology, Mandatum, and Prudential Judgments," *Pro Ecclesia* 11, no. 1 (Winter 2002): 20–23. On the basis of this theological discourse of "full communion," some theologians reflected on *Ex Corde*'s negative impact on the ability of the church and its theologians to model a community of collaboration between employers and laborers, recommended in the church's own social teachings on the dignity and rights of labor. See Patrick T. McCormick, "Theology as Work: The Mandatum and the Rights of Labor," *Horizons* 29, no. 1 (Spring 2002): 128–34.

or approbation by church authority,' what exactly is the significance of the mandatum? Why would I need a mandatum from a bishop to teach in my own name?"[19]

Catholic feminist theologians and scholars in religious studies surprisingly share much common ground with *Ex Corde Ecclesiae*. In this apostolic constitution on the mission and identity of Catholic colleges and universities,[20] the late Pope John Paul II emphasized an integral interconnection between critical scholarly work and academic freedom in the pursuit of the truth, human rights, and the common good (ECE par. 12; cf. Art 2 n. 5); urged interdisciplinary work to develop more adequate theology regarding social, economic, political, and ecological justice (ECE pars. 19, 32, 34, 40, 49); and affirmed the integrity and autonomy of theological methods to achieve the aforementioned goals (ECE par. 29)—all hallmarks of feminist methods and goals in theology and religious studies. In keeping with papal views and with their own methods and goals, feminist theologians still assent to definitive doctrine and church teaching as well as maintain accountability to the wider people of God.[21] Yet, some feminist theologians increasingly find themselves on the outs with some Catholic colleges.

In July 2008, the University of San Diego rescinded its invitation to Rosemary Radford Ruether to hold a major chair in theology,[22] which emphasizes the increasing fragility of academic freedom for feminist theology and studies in religion within some, certainly not all, Catholic

19. Robert J. Egan, "The Mandatum: Now What?" *Commonweal* 129, no. 7 (April 5, 2002): 14–19.

20. John Paul II, *Ex Corde Ecclesiae: Apostolic Constitution on Catholic Universities* (Rome: Libreria Editrice Vaticana, August 15, 1990), available at http://www.vatican.va/holy_ father/john_paul_ii/ apost_constitutions/ documents/hf_jp-ii_apc_15081990_ ex-corde ecclesiae_en.html.

21. For examples of such common theological responses to *Ex Corde*, see Catherine Mowry LaCugna, "Some Theological Reflections on *Ex Corde Ecclesiae*," in *The Challenge and Promise of a Catholic University*, ed. Theodore M. Hesburgh (Notre Dame, IN: University of Notre Dame Press, 1994), 117–25; Daniel C. Maguire, "Academic Freedom and the Vatican's *Ex Corde Ecclesiae*," *Academe* (May/June 2002); Richard P. McBrien, "Academic Freedom and the Catholic Theologian," in *Issues in Academic Freedom*, ed. George S. Worgul Jr. (Pittsburgh: Duqesne University Press, 1992), 126–42; and, idem, "Theologians at Risk? *Ex Corde* and Catholic Colleges," *Academe* (Jan/Feb 2001).

22. Scott Jaschik, "Theologian Uninvited to Hold Chair," *Inside Higher Education*, July 21, 2008, available at www.insidehighered.com/news/2008/07/21/usd.

institutions of higher education. According to widespread reports, the USD provost withdrew Ruether's already accepted and announced appointment on ideological grounds, i.e., the donor's vision of the chair did not match Ruether's theological writings or political practices. Some grassroots feminist organizations quickly formulated a petition with nearly 2,200 signatories that described these events and defended the academic freedom of Catholic feminists on the grounds of the current pope's speech in April 2008, which upheld "the great value of academic freedom. In virtue of this freedom you are called to search for the truth wherever careful analysis of evidence leads you." The petition also argued for academic freedom on the theological grounds of the rich diversity in the Catholic intellectual tradition.[23] Recognizing a more elastic than monolithic definition of academic freedom, the signatories offered their own constructive theology of academic freedom, grounded in equal creation in the *imago Dei*, feminist theological method that prioritizes learning from women's experience about more universally shared human dilemmas and desires, and scriptural encounters between women and Jesus, which compelled him toward a more expansive ministry. A feminist theology of academic freedom, in my view, might also be based on the dynamics of grace—a *freedom from* political and religious pressures that reflect only a partial understanding of the issues[24] and a *freedom for* creative and constructive theological thought, practice, and life that is accountable to Catholic tradition as well as women's experiences with that tradition, for good and for ill.

These two perspectives manifest, respectively, different relationships between faith and reason as well as between religion and culture. On the one hand, the magisterial view entails an "impartial search for truth . . . that is neither subject to nor conditioned by particular interests of any kind" (ECE pars. 5, 7), except the magisterium's current concern with presenting an alternative to so-called secular culture.[25]

23. "Letter to the University of San Diego Supporting Academic Freedom and Rosemary Radford Ruether," August 21, 2008, available at www.ipetitions.com/petition/RRR_AcademicFreedom /index.html.

24. Hellwig expressed concerns about "self-appointed censors" in response to *Ex Corde* in Arlene Levinson, "Catholic Campuses Head for Showdown with U.S. Church: Academic Freedom vs. Loyalty," *The Gazette* (Montreal, Quebec) May 29, 2002: B8.

25. Several studies regarding the role of religion in U.S. higher education show the secularization thesis—or the sociological theory that modern Enlightenment-based

Addressing that concern partly involves requiring a mandatum in the case of all Catholic theologians teaching Catholic doctrine and morals within Catholic higher education (ECE Art. 4 n. 3, Art. 5 n. 1; cf. Appl. II, Art. 4, par. 4). On the other hand, a feminist theological view of academic freedom certainly involves faith-based convictions and research in service of the people of God and of society (ECE, par. 13). But, it also recognizes the value and possibly virtue of "ambivalence"[26] rather than unqualified "fidelity" and "conformity" (Appl. I, par. 7; II, Art. 2, par. 2) when it comes to matters of faith and morals regarding women, the poor, the earth, and other issues of social justice.

These two perspectives appear unlikely allies because feminist theology and studies in religion are often portrayed (branded, in the negative sense) as anathema to the institutional Catholic Church's pursuit of the common good. Indeed, feminism is sometimes signified amid a cluster of sociocultural trends that are opposed to Catholic faith and morals.[27]

Especially but not only feminist theologians counter such branding (in the negative sense) by reinventing the brand (in the marketing sense) of Catholic education itself. They imagine and enact new ways of being Catholic via articulating and embodying fresh theological constructions of doctrines, symbols, and practices for our times. In other words, feminist theologians and scholars in religious studies continue to "own" and reinvent the Catholic brand of higher education, acknowledging that their transformative work for a just and justice-oriented church and society at the cutting edge may well get them, like Ruether, cut out of religiously-affiliated educational institutions. Monika spilled much media and theological ink in the aftermath of *Ex Corde Ecclesiae* to point out that (1) the silence and absence of such voices strains the credibility of U.S. Catholic colleges and universities, and that (2) some

---

culture marginalizes religious beliefs, practices, and peoples—to run contrary to the actual rise of religious studies and students in academia. See, for example, Susan E. Henking, "Religion, Religious Studies, and Higher Education: Into the 21st Century," *Religious Studies Review* 30, nos. 2/3 (April/July 2004): 129–36.

26. Mary Farrell Bednarowski, *The Religious Imagination of American Women* (Indianapolis: Indiana University Press, 1999), esp. chap.1.

27. Eileen McNamara, "Linking Evil to Feminism," *Boston Globe*, April 11, 2004; Michael Paulson, "O'Malley Writes An Apology to Women: Feminism Remark, Foot-Washing Cited," *Boston Globe*, April 30, 2004; and, idem, "O'Malley Reflects, After Five Tumultuous Years," *Boston Globe*, August 3, 2008.

proposed measures of Catholic identity (e.g., loyalty oaths, Catholic majority on faculty and boards, etc.) potentially undermine U.S. federal aid to such institutions of higher education, because they may violate U.S. constitutionally protected religious freedoms.[28]

Beyond these practical and political points, I argue that pushing feminist and other cutting-edge theological voices to the periphery or altogether out of Catholic higher education damages rather than enhances its Catholic as well as its democratic character. Without the free exchange of diverse views, being "Catholic" narrows to an authoritarian, juridical, institutional notion of the church that trades on hierarchical relations of power and obedience for membership. As Monika contended in *Understanding Catholicism*, such an institutional model of the church forecloses on the notion of Catholic identity and tradition as a lived and living community of open critical and constructive discourse and practice, a whole people of God engaged in a free, faithful, reasoned, and inspirited exchange within and between groups, across generations, and around the globe about the ongoing truth and relevance of its organizing texts, beliefs (doctrinal and moral), symbols, and practices.[29] In the literature on public theology, both the church and U.S. civil society are construed as such communities of conversation.[30] Yet, current events in Catholic higher education show that such communities of genuine dialogue and deliberation (i.e., civil society) are jeopardized, thereby raising questions about the ability of such educational institutions to shape students for responsible religious and civic engagement. Wanting a more deliberative and consensus-building notion of the church

28. As summarized by Kate Zernike, "Catholic Colleges See Peril in Vatican Push for Control," *Boston Globe*, January 4, 1999: A1. Hellwig identified these issues in her comments regarding the U.S. Catholic bishops' second-round draft of practical procedures to implement *Ex Corde*. Quoted in Brooke A. Masters, "At Catholic Colleges, Higher Truths Collide; Scholars Fear Push for Loyalty to the Vatican," *Washington Post*, February 5, 1999: B1; and in James M. O'Neill, "Vatican Guidelines Stir Catholic Colleges; Bishops Are Meeting This Week in Hopes of Carving Out a Middle Ground," *Philadelphia Inquirer*, June 27, 1999: A3.

29. Hellwig, *Understanding Catholicism*, 2nd ed. (Mahweh, NJ: Paulist Press, 2002), esp. chap. 7. In non-Catholic theological circles, Christian identity and tradition as a community of argument is advocated by Kathryn Tanner, *Theories of Culture: A New Agenda for Theology* (Minneapolis: Fortress Press, 1997), 123–28, 151–55, and 172–75.

30. See Carbine, "Ekklesial Work," 436–40.

on college campuses does not imply making the authoritative teaching office of the church into a representational capitalist democracy. My point is that educational institutions insofar as they limit Wisdom's feast, i.e., prevent debate and deliberation among a rich range of diverse and disparate voices, Catholic and otherwise, might not shape students for responsible citizenship, for negotiating their religio-political identity in an increasingly pluralistic U.S. public realm.

In keeping with Monika's work on reconciling public virtues that I have discussed above in relation to the biblical Wisdom tradition, being Catholic goes beyond the binary of either obedient loyalty or conscientious dissent to the church hierarchy. As sociological studies of pro-change U.S. Catholics demonstrate, being Catholic means negotiating religious identity in ecclesial, academic, and political publics. It means belonging to a religious community of shared memory and moral conviction that creatively mines and appropriates its traditions (institutional, doctrinal, symbolic, ritual) to maintain religious identity and to effect change in society and in the church.[31] There is hope for reclaiming a feminist perspective on academic freedom within Catholic higher education. This is not a simple dichotomy between institutional and individual academic freedom, in which institutional freedom to express Catholic identity trumps individual freedom to critically and creatively engage that identity. Rather, magisterial and feminist notions of academic freedom are not incommensurable because both desire Wisdom, the divine presence, and the common good.

In his address to Catholic educators in April 2008, Pope Benedict XVI interpreted all teachers (bishops and laity alike) as bearers of Wisdom, which holds much promise for Catholic higher education given that feminist theologians and theological educators also retrieve the Wisdom tradition as discussed above. The current pope also equated the religious identity of Catholic colleges and universities not with student or faculty religious profiles or curricular orthodoxy (as suggested in the *Application of* Ex Corde), but with an educational site for the incarnation, for encountering and recognizing the divine presence in liturgy, in justice, and in creation—all of which resonates with feminist

---

31. Michele Dillon, *Catholic Identity: Balancing Reason, Faith, and Power* (New York: Cambridge University Press, 1999).

theological concerns for doing "saving work"[32] in service to imagining and at least beginning to create a better, alternate world than one shaped by rugged individualism, elite entitlement and greed, and the abuse of the ecological environment. Feminist theologians and scholars of religion, thus, might find some unlikely fertile ground in Monika's example as a messenger of Wisdom and in contemporary magisterial pedagogy on which to build an alternate—and perhaps no longer opposite—theory and practice of academic freedom within the realm of the Catholic intellectual tradition. Looking at Catholic higher education through the Wisdom tradition and its representatives like Monika may even enable what *Ex Corde* intended—to provide an opportunity to assess how Catholic colleges and universities communicate and imbue their mission to students.

In reflecting on my own ten years in teaching theology and religious studies to undergraduate and graduate students at religiously affiliated and inspired institutions of higher education, I find myself applying what Monika described as the Catholic tradition to my own vocation as feminist theological educator. In her book *Understanding Catholicism*, Monika characterized the Catholic tradition as a conversation between faith-filled belief and practice on the one hand and reasoned inquiry about those beliefs and practices in each new era on the other hand. As a messenger of Wisdom, Monika invited—not coerced—her students to that conversation table in order to ask the "far-reaching, dangerous, frightening . . . urgent questions having to do with the public, political and economic dimensions"[33] of our shared common life, and thereby walk in the way of insight. My hope is that my own teaching emulates a small spark of Monika's invitation to that table in order to mutually enrich the Catholic tradition, students of it, and our society.

---

32. Rebecca S. Chopp, *Saving Work: Feminist Practices of Theological Education* (Louisville, KY: Westminster John Knox, 1995).

33. Hellwig, *Understanding Catholicism*, 1–5, esp. 4–5.

Because the challenges of war, famine, huge refugee populations, increasing political polarizations, and pervasive injustices in the world are so large, it is very tempting to conclude that it is beyond our scope to act, and that our only contribution can be prayer. But prayer itself is, of course, for our own transformation and empowerment by grace to live, relate, and act according to the wisdom of the Reign of God.

— remarks of Monika Hellwig on
receipt of the *Populorum Progressio*
Award, 2004, read by Dr. Fred Leone

Chapter 5

Monika Hellwig and Christian Life Communities at Georgetown University

Lee Nelles Leonhardy

What a heady, humbling, and enriching privilege to have known Monika Hellwig—and to have been with her in an intimate and informal environment at least once or twice a month. That was the circumstance that about ten of us have enjoyed, with Monika present for more than twelve of our sixteen years of gathering.

Additionally there was the benefit of being with other people who also prized this opportunity and had common interests—intellectual, spiritual—grounded in a generosity of humanity. Monika obviously made a determined effort to attend as many of the biweekly meetings as possible, and would greet us with "Hello, everyone! Sorry I'm late!" and a big smile. It was always a remarkable meeting, with many paths to follow.

We appreciated every minute. Of course, all of us, being of a certain age and embracing realism, knew that no situation is static. We were conscious that our situations can change. But even in 2005, such a severe change as losing Monika had not seemed to be forecast in the short-term for our group and our long-term association with her.

We were, and still are, members of the Georgetown University CLC, our origins reflecting, through Monika, the international organization of Christian Life Communities. However, we are not and never were formally affiliated with the larger organization of the same name.

Monika was open to many things and had learned of the CLC organization back in the late 1980s and found it appealing. She joined a neighborhood group in Silver Spring, Maryland, headed by the president of the national association, Fred Leone. Monika attended meetings of the Silver Spring group even after starting CLC at Georgetown University.

Christian Life Communities, with its underpinnings of Ignatian spirituality and the Spiritual Exercises, was the worldwide successor to the Sodality organization. It reflected the Vatican II dimension of the call to community life, which would echo Monika's enthusiasm for the council. Even before she was a CLC member, she had written some articles on community spirituality for its national and world publications.

Early Georgetown University CLC Connections

Although opportunities for spiritual exploration existed on the Georgetown University campus in the early 1990s, it was Monika's nature to be aware that others were looking, consciously or unconsciously, for a variety of accessible spiritual anchors. She sensed the need for faith and prayer, intimacy with God, to be integrated into campus daily life. Monika's vision was expansive. Because of who she was, with her giving and sharing nature, she believed that a variety of opportunities oriented toward spirituality should be readily accessible to members of the Georgetown University community. By being where she was, with her contacts and experiences, she was able to evaluate many possibilities and opportunities for bringing people together to meld faith into their daily lives.

Apparently, by 1993, Monika had decided that the CLC group model was an appropriate vehicle to bring to the campus. It would be a means for graduate students, faculty, and staff to experience enhanced spiritual awareness and involvement.

"Monika was always caring about everyone's spirituality," said Betty Smith, an original member of the Georgetown University Christian Life Community. She worked in the university library at the time. Betty remembers having lunch with Monika and Monika asked her, "What are you doing for your spiritual life?" Betty knew that "this type of personal interest in the spirituality of others was very much on Monika's mind. She was a very human and a very concerned woman."[1]

---

1. Betty Smith, CLC meeting, 28 April 2009; telephone interviews by author, and e-mail communications to author, April–August 2009. She and her husband, Roy, are still members of CLC.

In 1993, at a CLC conference at Marquette University, Dr. Leone introduced Monika to Anthony Franchina, just moving from Ohio State to Georgetown to take a position with the office of the chaplain. Anthony recalls meeting several times with Monika at the conference, and after sharing a final supper there, she said to him, "I have been talking with the university chaplain for quite a while about starting some CLCs at Georgetown—but I couldn't do it by myself. I'll cover the administration and senior faculty, and you the junior faculty and graduate students—and we'll do it!"[2] Anthony agreed.

She got in touch with Joe Pettit, who was in university administration—they had known each other in the early 1960s when Monika, still in her religious order, was on the GU campus teaching linguistics to missionaries.[3] He agreed to join and was able to host one of the groups in his office on the main campus. Another called by Monika was Dr. John Collins Harvey of the Georgetown University Medical School, who had been associated with her in matters involving ethics and medical issues. He too became a CLC member.[4]

Monika's recruiting continued. She put a small ad about CLC in the faculty newspaper, *The Blue & Gray*, inviting interested faculty and staff members to inquire about CLC. Mary Lee Giblon Sheahan, of the Faculty of Languages and Linguistics, saw it, called, and then met with Monika. "I can still remember us sitting there, over coffee, and she explained to me the fundamentals of CLC. I liked her immediately—she was so open, so simple, so intellectually sharp. I thought, 'It doesn't sound wacky—with her guidance it should be okay, so I think I'll give it a try.' I joined shortly thereafter." She has been a member of the group ever since, along with her husband, Jack.[5]

The original two groups merged into one. Membership has been extremely stable over the years.

In 1997, I was asked to join the group. I welcomed the opportunity to be in a group devoted to topics such as spirituality and Vatican II. I

2. Anthony Franchina, e-mail communication to author, 31 July 2009.

3. Joseph Pettit, telephone interviews by author and e-mail communications to author, July–August 2009. He and his wife, Mary, are continuing members.

4. Dr. John Collins Harvey, telephone interviews by author and e-mail communications to author, July–August 2009.

5. Mary Lee Giblon-Sheahan, interviews by author, e-mail communications to author, and telephone conversations with author, April–August 2009.

was quite overwhelmed at the prospect of being part of an ongoing group with Monika Hellwig, a renowned theologian, lecturer, author, and faculty member. At that time I had not read a single one of her books. I had, however, attended one of her lectures and I had been very impressed, both by the lecture and the person. And my friends laughed at my reticence and said to come along.

At my first meeting, it was as if a new world opened—to meet regularly and frequently with like-minded individuals, all readers, all curious, all able to discuss *and* to listen, to muse about deep thoughts, express opinions, and frame questions, in an atmosphere of ease, acceptance, and trust. Monika's presence alone was inspiring. However, the members themselves had impressive backgrounds and demeanor. The atmosphere was not judgmental. One knew: it was a privilege to be there.

Privileged Meetings with Monika

From my initial meeting with Monika, I had such a sense of her "wholeness," of a complete person, one who observed the world both broadly and in close detail, who lived both in the "real" world and in the spiritual. She took given details and assembled them into her wise understanding of God's wholeness. Monika talked to us directly and from her accumulated knowledge of life, her wisdom.

Monika was able to express in a simple manner major ideas that others would have trouble expressing in paragraphs and pages. About her was a sense of order, of oneness. There was no chasm between the person she appeared to be and the truth of who she really was, between her own sense of her person and her understanding of the wholeness of God and God's world. Underlying all was warmth, nourishing warmth.

Her friendship with God was reflected in her entire person. Monika really believed that the church is alive through its people. Someone once teased her about "hanging out with the intellectuals" and teaching philosophy and theology and then coming to us, and asked her why she would spend her time with us. She responded, "I love it—it brings a balance to my life!"

Monika made it clear she wanted to be a "member" of the group, to be part of the group. She did not want to be the leader, which is why she encouraged us to assume that responsibility on a meeting-to-meeting basis. To all present, however, it was readily apparent that everyone in the group looked to Monika for guidance and in many ways. Nevertheless, she saw part of her role as instilling confidence and enabling us as Christians to be able to speak about our faith, independently of her.

With Monika it seemed no question was too basic, too simple, too complex, or too unwieldy to talk about forthrightly and to analyze. Yet she was not a debater. There was never a "put down." She was a steady person, always open and always reflective. There was succinctness about her person and her character. She was impatient with fuzzy thinking in any venue, and especially within hierarchical circles.

She was the quiet authority, certainly our spiritual guide. But she wanted us to grow and would say, "Never be afraid of making a mistake." Monika gave us the opportunity to think clearly about our spiritual lives. This had a profound effect on us. From time to time she would pursue the line of "Here is what you said, and here is what I heard you say from a spiritual point of view."

Monika was an excellent judge of people and certainly sized us up accurately. When Monika attended, she would listen a large portion of the time while discussions continued. As one member hypothesized, perhaps some of Monika's quiet calmness during these sometimes-vigorous discussions reflected the peace of one who has no need to prove anything.

Then, as now, the group's support or advice is warm, wise, sometimes witty, always wholehearted and good-hearted, and very caring. The responses reflect positive principles and beliefs, sometimes with commentary, often lightened by levity. Monika and all of us shared openly. All the members of the group have felt they could express many different kinds of views.

As time and trust developed, Monika obviously felt she could share personal issues also. She would mention family problems, physical and mental health issues. With all that she had seen, suffered, and survived (beginning with deep personal tragedies relating to WWII, followed by other events), she never gave any hint of having been a "victim," nor could we ever imagine her accepting "victimhood." It seemed important for her to share her lay spirituality with our group. Her own openness, her reflective nature, her steadiness always set the standard.

The original members of the group have said that Monika made it clear that she was "one of us." There existed a very nonjudgmental atmosphere (as there is today). Within a short time, Monika came to confide in the group as with a trusted friend. She would admit there were problems for her and we became a source of consolation and support for her. Of course, this happened because there had been built this ambience of trust and confidence. We had all brought knotty personal situations to the table. It was quite humbling when she would bring up problems with her family and see us, parents also, as a sounding board. She did not actively say she was looking for answers but she was always listening and considering our words and thoughts. We felt that in some measure we could give back to her on a very personal level, as she gave to us. Her demeanor was always reserved but there were many times in the later years when she would look very tired, even though her upbeat smile was always in evidence. We particularly wanted to offer her comfort.

Monika's Wisdom

Monika was wise, and her extensive knowledge was the underpinning for that wisdom. She generously, but never intrusively, gave us the benefit of her understanding and wisdom of what is good and what is not, on many levels.

Monika's witnessing the Second Vatican Council was pivotal in her history and she wanted it to be understood and truly important to others. She took the dynamics and the results in fully and wanted to bring others into a similar degree of understanding.

"Monika was a great champion of Vatican II and was very sympathetic to what transpired. She wanted to make sure Vatican II was going to guide us. These were tremendous changes and she gave us so much more of an understanding than we've gotten anywhere else. I think many of us have changed our views."[6]

She wanted us to grow into a Vatican II church, a postconciliar church. For those of us searching, Monika tried to show this group, with the emphasis on Vatican II, that there was a "new way of being Catholic." There was the acknowledgment that there has been a slow coming out of what had been the church of our childhood.

6. John Harvey, telephone interview by author and e-mail communications to author, April–August 2009.

Frequently our discussions would touch on issues of morality, compassion, societal responsibility, political accountability, and controversial policies. Through her questions, she would cast the discussion with reference to Vatican II thought. She was able to express major ideas so simply that you understood easily and realized there were alternative ways of thinking about and approaching issues that you might have considered set.

Her being the expert witness for many aspects of our discussions would lead her to comment on how words or phrases could have unique connotations when used in Scripture or other texts, especially historical ones, with different authors and in different traditions and time periods. Her great strength was in not just giving these to us complete and *gratis*, but in giving us enough information so we could tease out conclusions of our own. Occasionally, Monika would take us on short detours through different times, in order to explain some issue she felt important for us to understand.

Her knowledge of history was extraordinary. And she could, clearly and cleanly in just a few measured words and phrases, analyze and present a concise picture of a broad range of times, places, and persons. Without ever seeming ponderous or rushed, she often would throw some small intimate detail into a discussion, which would make the point of the universality of human emotions, intent, and actions. This was especially true of situations relating to her presence or role in a particular process. For example, when she became president of the Association of Catholic Colleges and Universities and went to meetings in the Vatican, she would return and relate to us what had happened, the inner workings of meetings, and especially her part in the discussions. In one instance, she described how she drew out for her listeners the obvious conclusions if a particular policy were to be put into effect, leading to potential results no one else had been willing to put forth or examine. We avidly listened and, if we had questions, she would answer very clearly. She gave to us a sense of intimacy with the situations in which she had a part.

Monika would give unique insight into governance actualities within the church, past and present. She had a practical working knowledge of the policy formation, protocols, and intrigues in the Vatican, having been intimately involved in Vatican II and subsequent gatherings there, whether formal, intimate, off-the-record, or casual. The accumulation of her experiences, her calm, mild aura of authority, and her memory and analysis of those experiences were—not to exaggerate—phenomenal.

We would say things such as, "I never understood how such and such a policy came out of the Vatican." This would lead to helpful discussions. With her extensive exposure to ecclesial doings on every level, Monika shared enough information so we could come to conclusions on our own. She could also give us details of events that occurred in closed settings and that had a bearing on final decisions.

"One of Monika's many talents was to create an atmosphere where we could explore our faith in an open manner, in a nonthreatening way, giving us a confidence to speak out, with all of us knowing that nothing would go out of the four walls of that room."[7] We prize the sense of confidentiality among us.

This kind and level of sharing of one's faith reality and deep personal needs (whether family, career, or other) may not be the desired norm for many. Nor is the willingness to challenge one's levels of beliefs or knowledge likely to be the stuff of the majority. Upon reflection, we have to consider whether it was Monika's confidence and lack of fear that led us to have confidence in our growth, greater understanding, and a desire for a long-lasting and developing spiritual journey. Monika believed, "Pray and it will come to you," that we are catalysts for God's power. We always have a book under discussion. In the early days of meeting and while she was still on campus as a faculty member, Monika usually chose the books. As she became busier and traveled more in her position with Catholic colleges and universities, but was still able to attend from time to time, she would frequently suggest a book. In this way she introduced us to many authors whose work we have prized. (See attached bibliography.)

Monika seemed amazingly skilled in shepherding discussions through logical steps to reasonable conclusions, employing the clear sort of progression and lucidity where, at the conclusion, you want to slap your forehead, and say, "Why couldn't I have seen that, or thought of that?" If someone got something wrong, she very gently would bring into the conversation the pertinent references to inform all of us of the correct information.

Monika had a very broad perspective. With her as a guide, we raised many questions of history or policy that covered a wide range of uni-

7. Mary Lee Giblon-Sheahan, April–August 2009.

versal church matters. Such queries would be broad or detailed, factual or speculative. One member has said, "I came always to listen to her wisdom and enormous knowledge."[8]

Monika herself was a very attentive listener, and seemed to like to hear personal viewpoints expressed. And she would ask questions if she wanted clarification of an opinion or point of discussion. Her forte was in understanding the dynamics of human behavior as related to the spiritual, whether in a family setting, a university, a political venue, a parish, or the church.

She was always happy to give an explanation or exegesis. For example, she helped set the story of Jesus back in its own time, looking at customs of the Jewish people then. "She would explain symbolism and allegories so they gave a much bigger picture."[9] Her answers to inquiries sometimes took the form of a beautifully phrased return question designed to pique a creative response.

Without Monika's input the discussion could and can go in a persistent tangential direction. When she was present, in her crisp yet inclusive way she always seemed delighted to give explanation, exegesis, and human interest anecdotes to get us back on track.

To sustain such taxing endeavors, group members bring coffee and snacks, some simple, some elaborate, some healthful, some not. When Monika attended, we always enjoyed the contents of her fresh box of ginger cookies.

One of our members, Jack Sheahan, had known Monika for a long time and was always struck by her modesty. One night when he was talking to her, he quoted a passage from a book she had written in 1986. She looked at him and then exclaimed, "I can't believe I wrote that!"[10]

Before she came to her first meeting, another member was quite excited about meeting *the* Monika Hellwig. Many years previously, although she had never before heard of the author, she had bought and read Monika's book on the sacrament of penance. It completely changed her attitude toward the sacrament. "I found it was just what I needed

---

8. Othmar Winkler, CLC meeting, 28 April 2009; e-mail communications to author, and telephone conversations with author, April–August 2009.

9. Mary Lee Giblon-Sheahan, April–August 2009.

10. Jack Sheahan, CLC meeting, 28 April 2009; phone conversation with author, and e-mail communications to author, April–August 2009.

to learn and it changed my life. When invited to join CLC I couldn't believe our mentor would be Monika Hellwig. One night I told her how grateful I was because her book led me to a new understanding and to frequent celebration of the sacrament. I thanked her. She listened to me, with full attention, and finally quietly said, 'I am surprised. . . . But I am very glad.'"[11]

It is ironic that, probably in the spring of 2005, Joe Pettit commented at a meeting, when Monika was not present, that we had by no means read all or even many of Monika's books and "we really should be choosing her books so we can have her comments and insights. Her books have made a big impact on my life."[12] That hope of being able to work with Monika and her books together was not to be fulfilled.

The Group Today

The Christian Life Community at Georgetown today retains many of the original members from 1993, some of their spouses, and people invited by others in the group. It has an informal membership of about ten and has now been meeting for sixteen years, the first twelve years with Monika's active participation. The group has gathered regularly, approximately twice a month during the university school year.

Obviously our time with Monika affected all of us very positively. We recognize and celebrate that such a time was made available to us, and, of course, there is mourning for the loss. With her sense of realism as well as her spirituality and the gifts she showered on us, Monika surely would have expected us to continue to meet. And indeed we have. Our group has its own identity. Being with each other has been highly rewarding. Probably none of us had any serious thought of not continuing after she died. We make every effort to continue, as before, with the same openness and willingness to probe issues and to ask for help in understanding.

We acknowledge that we do not have the ability to question and find answers with the same authority of knowledge that Monika gave us. Our discussions today do not conclude with the same sense of satisfaction as when we had our "higher authority" in house. None of us

---

11. Eliane Raine, e-mail communication to author, 27 July 2009.
12. Joe Pettit, July–August 2009.

is a theologian, church historian, biblical scholar, or highly knowledgeable in contemporary developments of ecclesial policy, and yet we choose books on subjects that challenge our interests in these related fields.

We select books we think are appropriate and worthwhile, to tackle serious works with enthusiasm, to join in prayer and sharing, and to exercise the heritage Monika gave us.

We prize the continuity and compatibility of our group and, perhaps more than anything, we prize the common bond of faith, our history during and after our time with Monika, and our notable trust and confidence in each other. Our membership has been stable for many years, but we recognize exclusivity can stultify new growth and interests. That also is to be considered.

Perhaps some of our charism will be found in some of the social works of Monika, to pass on to others her compassion and wisdom to the extent that we can.

Life with Monika was vital, challenging, wondrous, surprising, generous, caring, kind, concerned, full of breadth and depth. That is certainly irreplaceable. As with any group, growth is now for us to nurture. The constancy we have demonstrated over the last four years reflects the confidence given us by Monika, the promotion and development by her of our independence.

Our gratitude is boundless and endless.

Georgetown CLC Bibliography

Barry, William. *Contemplatives in Action*. Mahwah, NJ: Paulist Press, 2002.

D'Antonio, William, James Davidson, Dean Hoge, and Mary Gautier. *American Catholics Today*. Lanham, MD: Rowman & Littlefield Publishers, Inc., 2007.

DeMello, Anthony. *Contact with God*. Chicago: Loyola Press, 1991.

Hellwig, Monika. *Public Dimensions of a Believer's Life*. Lanham, MD: Rowman & Littlefield Publishers, Inc., 2005.

———. *Understanding Catholicism*. Mahwah, NJ: Paulist Press, 1981.

———. *What Are They Saying About Death and Christian Hope?* Mahwah, NJ: Paulist Press, 1979.

Magee, Peter. *God's Mercy Revealed*. Cincinnati, OH: St. Anthony Messenger Press, 2005.

Massaro, Thomas. *Living Justice: Catholic Social Teaching in Action*. Lanham, MD: Rowman & Littlefield Publishers, Inc., 2000.

Nolan, Albert. *Jesus Before Christianity*. Maryknoll, NY: Orbis Books, 1976.

———. *Jesus Today: A Spirituality of Radical Freedom*. Maryknoll, NY: Orbis Books, 2006.

Pope Benedict XVI. *Jesus of Nazareth*. New York, NY: Doubleday & Co., 2007.

Reiser, William. *To Hear God's Word, Listen to the World: The Liberation of Spirituality*. Mahwah, NJ: Paulist Press, 1997.

Underhill, Evelyn. *Abba*. Harrisburg, PA: Morehouse Publishing. 1982.

———. *The School of Charity*. Harrisburg, PA: Morehouse Publishing, 1991. (Originally: London: Longmans, Green & Co., 1934.)

———. *The Spiritual Life*. Harrisburg, PA: Morehouse Publishing, 1991. (Originally: London: Hodder & Stoughton, 1937.)

———. *The Ways of the Spirit*. Chestnut Ridge, NY: Crossroad Publishing Co., 2001.

Pentecost

I am not very sure if earth went up to heaven
Or heaven came down that day.
I only know that we were as men who drank new wine
And the divine lost its distance.
The day the rafters shook and everywhere you'd look
The flames were darting. I am not very sure
Whether the fire came out of me or flickered in, but this
    I know
That everywhere I go the smoldering embers wait to burst
    aflame
The earth is not the same and I am not the same, but as
    you might say
Mad, and burning up with fever, whetted keen
To make the earth burn too to see what I have seen.

—unpublished poem by Monika K. Hellwig;
given to John C. Haughey, SJ,
by Monika's sister Marianne

Chapter 6

The Catholicity of Monika Hellwig

John C. Haughey, SJ

M onika's many books do not capture what I believe was distinctive about her as a theologian, which I would like to elaborate on in this chapter. What impressed me about the woman I knew and admired cannot be caught with one descriptor so I will name and explain three of them. One was the range of her oversight and the insights she brought to each subject. She was nothing short of *episcopal*. Two, she was *whole*. Three, she was critically, inclusively *catholic*. No one of these alone satisfies me; together they do. But each needs some explanation to do justice to her ever-enlarging horizon of concerns moved by what Bernard Lonergan would have called "a catholicity of spirit/Spirit."

When I describe her as episcopal I am not thinking of her as a bishop or as an administrator. Rather, she functioned as an overseer of the worlds of theology and pastoral care, of doctrine and praxis, of people and the things of nature. She did so without election or appointment by the church. She was a shepherd of those who needed shepherding and a corrector of those who needed correcting (including me at times), without any ecclesial anointing having been done unto her other than baptism. Since she did not hold the office, one could ask what qualified her for these functions. I believe she housed the charism of overseer. Or put it this way: she learned to grow into the role of overseer by being a careful steward of the mysteries of God. I can say this with some authority, not because I knew her as a result of her teaching at Georgetown University or because we shared the same dais at times or because we were close friends. Rather, I knew her in a more intimate way because I directed her in her full use of the Spiritual Exercises of St. Ignatius. It was then that I became very aware of the depth of her stewardship of the mysteries of God.

To take just one example of her stewarding these mysteries from her writings: she wrote a whole book that developed from one integrating insight, namely, that God is the host and we are God's guests at the table of creation. She stressed the largesse of our host and the need for each of us guests to imitate the quality of host in our relations to one another around the table and, in turn, with all the creation from which this bounty has been mediated. And like an effective bishop would, she was careful to make sure that all the Creator's guests—that is, we and all of the *creata*—"are drawn into the conversation so that none feel excluded or unwanted and that all can contribute to the occasion."[1] How simple and inclusive even of ecology is her insight that we are all guests of God's hospitality.

To say that she was a whole person is more difficult to describe. There was something whole about how she lived, thought, prayed, wrote, and suffered. What is it that makes a person whole? To answer that question I feel the need to use one of the categories Bernard Lonergan used to articulate what makes a person whole. It was the category of meaning. He would say that someone would have to be able to access all the realms of meaning to be a whole person. The key idea here is that if someone is in touch with and is able to operate from the basic founts of meaning, one is likely to qualify as whole. To put this in terms of meaning presumes that the reader appreciates the fact that all of us live in a context that is mediated by meanings. To be unaware of this is to be meaning-ignorant and, therefore, likely to be a poor candidate for being a whole person.

To spell out the realms of meaning to which human beings should have access, these are common sense, transcendence, theory, and interiority.[2] Since these terms do not immediately convey their contents, an explanation of each is called for. After doing that I will show how Monika embodies each of them.

1. Monika K. Hellwig, *Guests of God: Stewards of Divine Creation* (Mahwah, NJ: Paulist Press, 1999), 11.

2. Bernard Lonergan, "Realms of Meaning," *The Lonergan Reader*, ed. Mark and Elizabeth Morelli (Toronto: University of Toronto Press, 1997), 466–70.

Common sense is something everyone has to grow in every day. Negotiating traffic, for instance, or cooking dinner or keeping one's bank account straight or bolting the door at night or making sure one's child is dressed for the day at school given the weather report—the list is endless. What all the items involve is stuff in relation to me and me to the stuff I have to deal with every day in a common-sense way. And what I didn't get right yesterday, I'll be more adept at dealing with tomorrow. Although many have already conferred a doctorate on themselves in this realm of practicality, the more self-aware know they will always remain ABD, all but done, in meriting such a credential. There will never be a time when this realm of meaning is irrelevant. But to be satisfied with living within the meanings coming from this fount will make for a narrow mind and small soul.

Transcendence, a second realm of meaning, is the world beyond the immanent. For most people this realm has its reality from their sense of God and whatever goes into that experience and belief. More abstractly, it is their account of the good to be done and for whom it should be done, as well as the truth to be known insofar as this is possible about this transcendent reality. This realm of meaning widens the horizon of the here and now to include the beyond of the here and now, however this is construed by the meaning maker. Awakening to the reality of God generates this as a realm of meaning. It can become alive by prayer or practices. It can also be an inactive realm generating little or no meaning.

The third realm of meaning, which is theory, generally took its rise from the entry of science onto the human scene. Common sense, which deals with the expectables, can take one only so far before one runs into the inexplicables. Questions get raised that go beyond the things as they matter to me or to us. They can be answered only by inquiring about how things are in themselves, independently of the knowing and meaning common sense generates. So if the biologist takes his child to the zoo, for example, and both behold the giraffe, the boy will wonder whether it bites or kicks while "his father will wonder how the skeletal, locomotive, digestive, vascular and nervous systems combine and interlock."[3] Huge swatches of technical language emerge from the realm of theory, all of it seeking to explain things in themselves that

3. Lonergan, *Method in Theology* (Toronto: University of Toronto Press, 1999), 83.

transcendence and common-sense meanings don't produce. When faith seeks to understand further, the larvae of inquiry begin to produce theological wings.

The final realm of meaning was not an unknown before the modern era's turn to the subject, but it was not as formal or distinct or deliberate a realm as it became with "Kierkegaard, Schopenhauer, Newman, Nietzsche, Blondel, the personalists, and the existentialists."[4] Lonergan calls this realm *interiority*. That's a good start since it has the knower go inside, having been impacted by the multiple contents that need to be internalized by the intending subject. The intending subject's own subjectivity is experienced as it intends objects, raises questions, entertains doubts, makes judgments. It is from this realm of meaning that one's own self is discovered, authenticity is attained, and measured choices made. Experience is experienced as me experiencing, understanding as me understanding, insight as me hatching it, judgment as me judging. Discernment is more likely if the intender is attentive enough to differentiate between one operation and another, for example, between experiencing something and understanding it.

Self-appropriation is maybe a better synonym than self-determination for this realm of meaning that is interiority because it requires the self to appropriate the meanings available from the other three realms of meaning into and through the prism of the self. If the realm of interiority is not taken into account, no reliable edition of one's self will ever be published. Instead, one will be unself-consciously a mélange of the meanings of common sense, transcendence, and theory. This fourth realm comes *from* me, stamped by me with the emerging self I am and continue to become.

Monika fits the descriptor whole, not because she was an educator, a mother, a scholar, an author, a recipient of thirty-two honorary degrees, the executive director of a national educational organization. Rather, in these roles and honors there was something distinctive about the way she went about each of them.

My interest here is in seeing Monika Hellwig as having accessed all four realms of meaning, hence living within the horizon of wholeness

---

4. Ibid., 316.

elaborated above. Take common sense, for example. Her son Michael, one of three children adopted by her, assures me that he didn't miss not having a father because his mother had made herself so adept at running a household in all its complexities, not to mention her savvy about raising him and his brother and sister, children of a different race than she. This is eloquent testimony about her common sense. This realm of meaning had to develop in her much faster than in other children since her natural family kept dodging the effects of World War II while she was still very young. She learned to become a kind of mother to her two younger sisters when at the age of nine she was sent off to Scotland from her home in the Netherlands.

Her common sense never left her. The last experience I had of it was a week before she died, when she came to our community at Woodstock for dinner. Not only had she figured out the complexities of parking at Georgetown when lesser souls would have found it impossible to sequester her old car into a very unpromising space, but she knew exactly when her two hours had expired and she had to move it even though she was at the center of an intense conversation with our guests at that moment. Since common sense is such an obvious and ubiquitous category, I needn't dwell on it here except to assure the reader she had it in spades, as all of her children and acquaintances can attest.

Transcendence as a realm of meaning comes easily to the child, whose capacities for wonder are usually large before the blight of rationality and analysis constricts them. Monika's own words: "A first memory of being taken to church, for what must have been Benediction of the Blessed Sacrament, is a memory of being totally overwhelmed by a sense of mystery, and carrying that sense about with me in the days that followed as a precious secret and a kind of personal possession." One senses a kind of nostalgia for those early days as she recalled them in one of her last unpublished writings. "In heavily Catholic Limburg in the Netherlands I experienced from the age of 6 to 9 a traditional peasant Catholicism in which Church was not separate from the day to day life of the small towns and villages. Church was the culture of the people. It shaped the calendar with colorful public observances of house to house processions through the streets and pageants and plays of saints' lives on their feasts and heaven and hell on Shrove Tuesday and drawing of one's 'gift' and 'fruit' of the Holy Spirit out of a basket at Pentecost, and much more. One was simply engulfed in it, swimming in it. It filled the universe as a frame of interpretation for *everything*, even when one did not advert to it."[5]

We all inherit some account of the good and the true from our earliest years. Monika certainly did from her Catholicism. She also was exposed to very different accounts of the good and the true. There was Hitler's Germany before the family moved to Holland. Further, she experienced Scotland, to which she was sent at the age of nine, to be very "presbyterian," in the sense of having less ceremony and mystery and visual assistance for her sense of transcendence than she preferred and had grown used to in Catholicism. But there was nothing parochial in her preference. She expressly stated her profound appreciation of alternate accounts of the good and the true, beginning with Jews (her grandparents), German Lutherans, Scottish Presbyterians, and English Anglicans, as well as from a very edifying "agnostic."[6]

She was sure that the most influential adults on her in those years in Britain were the childless Welsh couple, the Whales, who virtually adopted Monika and her two sisters when they found them in dire circumstances. Barrett Whale was in many ways the father she had lost in an accident when she was five. Barrett was a thoroughly agnostic man, though their love for one another was a glorious fit at that time for the childless man and the waif-like vagabond. Besides Barrett and his wife, many others she met in these early years—German Lutherans, English Anglicans, Scottish Presbyterians, mentioned above—all served to deepen her own growing sense of the unity that obtained in an ever-widening awareness of human difference.

If interiority as a realm of meaning is a process of appropriating the self as it finds itself in the unique circumstances that force one to think for oneself, Monika had much grist for the mill early in her life. Not only was she removed from her family at the age of nine but she was moved with her sisters from one boarding school to another. At times the three of them "suffered from malnutrition and sheer deep hunger and roamed neighboring woods stripping bark off trees to eat." As if that weren't enough, "we were very inadequately protected against

5. Both quotes from Hellwig, "An Evolving Vision of the Church," unpublished manuscript.

6. Hellwig, "The Mandalas Do Not Break: A Theological Autobiographical Essay," in *Journeys*, ed. Gregory Baum (Mahwah, NJ: Paulist Press, 1975), 117–46.

the cold of the winter in northern Scotland. We slept in unheated attics and the bowls of water in which we were supposed to wash in the morning often contained only ice."[7]

"One comes out of such a childhood [of plural mentors with plural world views and considerable hardship] with a certain sense of universality rather than allegiance to any particular group. I have always felt a strong affinity to the uprooted and the deprived, probably because I have never been able to see the status quo of any society as normative."[8] A stint of working with the degraded and dehumanized, mostly the Irish poor of Liverpool, gave her an appetite for working with, as she imagined, the even needier poor of India that she had heard about from the Medical Missionary Sisters who had worked there. So, at the age of twenty-two she joined them with the intention of serving the poor in the Indian subcontinent as a member of that religious congregation.

She began to have a taste for the realm of meaning that is theory even before she entered the convent. She had sought out and purchased the *Dialogues* of Plato at the age of thirteen and at the age of sixteen relished the theoretical debates about jurisprudence at the Liverpool Law School, from which she got her first graduate degree. She discovered how at home she was with Aristotle at nineteen. Though her early experience was that "Catholicism was life, not primarily a matter of going to church," she began to be discriminating about this "life." "It was in the early years of adult life that I began to think about Church as such rather than Catholic life. My understanding was based on two encyclical letters, *Mystici Corporis* and *Mediator Dei*."[9] She was not left all that peaceful with what she called "the in-or-out character" of the ecclesiology she read there since she had by this time found many role models for life who were not Catholic. More appealing to her were the early social encyclicals *Rerum Novarum* and *Quadragesimo Anno*, since they had invited her into thinking about the church and its mission in and for the world rather than as an institution over against the world.

Catholic is a mark of the church. It connotes an emergence in the direction of universality. But it is an eschatological mark. It conveys what

7. Ibid., 128–29.
8. Ibid., 129.
9. Hellwig, "An Evolving Vision."

the church will be much more accurately than what it is. And since it will be, it must at present have an openness, even an acknowledgement, of its "not yet" character while being faithful to the "already" known contours of the divine mystery. This combination of being wide-eyed but not naïve developed in Monika at an early age, as should be seen from the above remarks. She was continually enlarging her mind and heart for ideas and people of other faiths and even for those of no faith.

It was at the dockside after she hugged her mother goodbye on the way to Scotland with her two sisters that she became aware "at that moment that my own experience was valid knowledge and that I would have to live by it. New voices would only be normative for me in a very secondary and relative way."[10] If that was the insight she had about herself when she was nine, she was surely a prescient, precocious human being. Her early sheltered life was left on a shore that receded from view minute by minute. Although she would not have been able to articulate it at the time, there was sufficient depth in her self-appropriation by this time that she knew the difference between a normless anomie and an inclusivity that already has an organizing story to which new voices could be added without disquieting her.

Her experience as a religious was mixed. How she described this says a lot about her critical, inclusive catholicity. On the one hand, she came to love the liturgies she experienced as a religious. "We learned and chanted a great deal of the Gregorian music."[11] That aesthetic experience was a major influence in her love of the Catholic tradition. She and the sisters spent time preparing for their liturgies and therefore participated full bore in them. Consequently, she commented that when the skill of the presider as homilist and liturgist was positive, the result was "an unexpected bonus but by no means necessary" to make the liturgy meaningful.[12] This is a salient comment on how consoling the liturgy was all her life. But it was as a religious that she was bemused by how little dependence their liturgies had on the clergy.

On the other hand, there were some negative things about religious life, beginning with the novitiate. "That was the only time in my life that I had the experience of being literally destroyed by exhaustion and

10. Hellwig, "The Mandalas Do Not Break," 128.

11. Ibid., 137.

12. Ibid.

physical strain, doing things in totally inefficient ways because the person in charge was too unintelligent to organize it better or too insecure to accept suggestions."[13] She never got to India. The order realized what an intellectual talent they had in her and saw its usefulness for training their members.

Her vocation to religious life was not permanent. After fourteen years she became a religious in the world, so to speak. She made two comments about her decision. "I am more sure that I followed my vocation in leaving than in joining the Society of Medical Missionaries."[14] Self-appropriation is never a finished project. Nor was it easy. "The institutional pressures were so strongly internalized in me that it was very difficult for me to conceive of fidelity in other than rather simplistic institutional terms."[15]

She had two stints of study at The Catholic University of America, one while still a nun, the other after that as a layperson doing her doctoral work. About the first stint she has a negative comment. "I was amazed to find it [the theology she was sent to study at Catholic University in Washington] so provincial."[16] In a word, it lacked the catholicity she had come to live. More specifically, the narrowness was in the curriculum. She commented that "the general assumption seemed to be that a liberal education could be very specifically defined in a more or less standard curriculum, and that theology was something that came after philosophy which was also defined by a specific sequence of courses that totally excluded most of the great thinkers in the world's history." She went on: "In terms of my background, everything that I learned could only appear as one strand of thought or experience among many others, each justified only in terms of its own frame of reference."[17] She found several happy exceptions to this narrowness: Frs. Gerard Sloyan and Godfrey Diekmann, OSB.

Then came the Second Vatican Council and, being the brightest thing the order had (I would presume), she was sent to live in Rome during it to assist a Vatican official with something connected to the

---

13. Ibid., 136.
14. Ibid., 143.
15. Ibid.
16. Ibid., 139.
17. Ibid., 139–40.

council. She never explained who he was or what her task was. What she did explain was the overwhelming intellectual conversion she felt by being a participant in and part of that event. It was about this event that she wrote her poem "Pentecost." It captures something of "the before and after" of her soul. While there she lived at the residence of the Movement for a Better World and was privy to many of the conversations and presentations made after hours by some of the council's *periti*, both at that residence and around Rome. She had already come to love and identify with the Catholic intellectual tradition but would not have guessed at the fuller dimensions of it until that gathering of the church between 1962 and 1965. Nothing stayed the same after her experience of the council. Now she knew that her life was to serve God's people by understanding God better and better through theology.

Naturally, her doctoral studies enabled her to see more deeply into these deeper dimensions of Catholicism. Although she came to love theology, she wasn't led astray by making it substitute for interiority. "The art that is theology consists in interpreting the symbols inherited within a tradition." These symbols are "accepted by those who live within the tradition as offering continuity, inner coherence and an adequate and appropriate response to contemporary questions about human life."[18] She didn't have to imagine this way of doing theology, since she found it in those who had deeply influenced the Vatican Council: Yves Congar, Karl Rahner, Edward Schillebeeckx, Barnabas Ahern, Bernard Haring. What had impressed her "was their colossal patience in mediating between the pastoral and the scholarly exigencies of any question under discussion." Consequently, "I could not think of theology as an elitist university game."[19] Furthermore, "for me it is not a career I have chosen but a task that somehow landed in front of me to be done . . . and done primarily from the resources of my own life experience within a great tradition that I am very happy to have internalized." And "for this tradition I have the deepest affection and respect . . . and for it I consider myself co-responsible."[20]

About the symbolic side of theology, its aesthetic, nonrational, experiential aspects were greatly expanded and legitimated by a course

18. Ibid., 143.
19. Ibid., 142.
20. Ibid., 145.

she took at the University of Pennsylvania in Indian iconography. "It opened my eyes for the first time to the symbolism of my own tradition."[21] Since the mandala was at the core of this experience for her and since the mandala has a fairly wide usage, I will surmise that what she meant by that term was some symbolic representation of her own worldview, one that included her sense of who God was and her place in that intuited theandric cosmo-vision. "My own mandala began to become visible to me in these classes, and ever since then I have seen mandalas emerging and diverging and converging in people's lives and in various traditions."[22]

These mandalas "don't break," as she put it, under the weight of the tragedies and ills that flesh is heir to, ills that she had been pierced by. But it seems that for her they are also in part inherited, "made of the cumulative vision and wisdom of many generations."[23] In brief, they visually construe a whole that captures the idiosyncrasy of the person vis-à-vis his or her tradition. Although she doesn't say as much, it seems obvious that her mandala was intimately connected to her Jewish grandparents since they were a major part of why her doctorate was on the literature of postbiblical religious Judaism. She found it "a thrilling and deeply satisfying experience."[24] She couldn't leave out her past, beginning with her own genes, in her construction of the whole that her mandala captured.

So the first article she published in theology[25] is even more interesting for supplying evidence of why it is apropos to characterize her interiority in terms of this virtue of catholicity. The theme is covenant. Since the unique subjectivity of an author does not leave the subject matter where it was in the literature, neither does she. There is a dynamism in consciousness that is intent on making wholes that impact it as disjoined parts. She would have no part of that. According to the catechesis she had been formed in, the covenant that Israel had received was taken to be abrogated and the new covenant Jesus made possible by his death

21. Ibid., 141.
22. Ibid.
23. Ibid., 141.
24. Ibid., 145.
25. Hellwig, "Christian Theology and the Covenant of Israel" in *Journal of Ecumenical Studies* (Winter 1970): 37–51.

superseded it. That dichotomous way of thinking fell short of the inclusivity she had learned from the council *periti* and had come to live by. Hence her doctoral dissertation's thesis, "A Proposal Towards a Theology of Israel as a Faith Community Contemporary with the Christian."

In it, Monika allows herself to enter into the experience of "contemporary Judaism's" relationship to the covenant and "to its worship of the one God as a witness to the nations." She had come to know firsthand "men experiencing a great fulfillment and happiness and purposefulness of life because they had become participants in the wisdom and creative joy of God."[26] She of course develops a sophistication about the covenant, but suffice it to say that she revisits Jesus' "new covenant in my blood" and grounds its meaning in thoroughly Old Testament terms. Furthermore, she foresees a time when there will be a doctrinal development in which there are three different faith communities (Islam, Judaism, and Christianity) functioning in a simultaneous and complementary participation in the same covenant. Granted, at present they are competing with each other "for unifying all mankind in the worship of the one God,"[27] but that will not continue to be so. What is needed to get to this complementarity, according to Monika, is a new understanding of revelation and a deeper grasp of the eschatological nature of the coming of the Messiah to the whole world.

In all of these very particular episodes she displayed a catholicity of spirit. Lonergan wrote an essay about the two different ways one can be Catholic. One of these is by being substantially one with other Catholics and Catholicism. The other is by being one with Christ in one's own subjectivity. In this second way one is "catholic with the catholicity of the Spirit of the Lord."[28] He wasn't being abstract by using this expression but specific about here-and-now personal living with its very concrete questions and solutions to questions that one has "thought out in Christ Jesus"[29] with the help of the indwelling Spirit. Here we are coming to the causality that explains the catholicity of Monika's interiority.

26. Hellwig, PhD thesis, The Catholic University of America, 1968, 45.

27. Ibid., 46.

28. Bernard Lonergan, *Existenz and Aggiornament* (Toronto: Regis College, 1965), 231.

29. Ibid.

I don't believe we can get to the taproot of Monika's catholicity unless we can find how her understanding of Christ evolved from what is technically called a high Christology to a low, ascending, historical one. The longer she experienced the church's authority, the more she appreciated Jesus' handling of the authority questions that pervaded his ministry. She notes, "he does not seem to hand over to his followers ready-made patterns to be implemented forever because of their coming from him." Rather, he communicated "his own heuristic methods in his quest for the reign of God. This has far-reaching implications for Catholicism."[30]

It surely did for her.

Another way to locate this character of Monika's catholicity is the way James Fowler sees what he calls "faithing."[31] He doesn't treat faith in terms of its contents or doctrines or even see it as necessarily religious. Rather he sees it as a universal human process and as having developmental stages in and through which the subject moves from an ego-centric condition to one that at its most mature stage he calls "a universalizing faith," which he deems rare. His structural approach to human development is like Piaget's and Kohlberg's. He smudges knowing, feeling, and valuing together under this rubric of faithing. What is most notable for our purposes in this chapter is the final or sixth stage, which Fowler calls universalizing faith. There is an inclusiveness to it; it includes "all being." In the previous stage, the fifth, the person experiences a paradoxical split between a transforming vision of love and justice and the untransformed world. In stage six, the split disappears because a unifying of this vision develops. Fowler describes Thomas Merton as an example of this unification. In Merton's last months of life he had an experience of looking at the giant Buddhas at Polonnaruwa wherein the paradox was transcended.

Fowler's explanation of this rare apogee of inclusionary faithing is what I and others who had the good fortune to know her found in Monika. There was such an intelligence and predisposition to hear and understand the other, a capaciousness in her own mandala that could

30. Hellwig, "On Rescuing the Humanity of Jesus: Implications for Catholicism" in *Open Catholicism: The Tradition at Its Best*, ed. David Efroymson and John Raines (Collegeville, MN: Liturgical Press, 1997), 48.

31. James W. Fowler, *Stages of Faith* (New York: Harper & Row, 1981).

make sense of the unexpected. She reverenced otherness and never foreclosed on an alternative voice if she could see its value, even voices that poorly worded their point or couldn't express their need. Parenting is probably a good condition for deepening the catholicity we have described here. She never ceased parenting—in triplicate, you might say.

There is an incident that I remember vividly in which the contrast between Monika's catholicity and those without such an excellence stood out. It was an event sponsored by the Ave Maria Law School at the National Press Club in Washington DC in October 2004. Its timing was masterfully calculated since it took place two weeks before the presidential election of that year. The invited audience was clearly of one persuasion, anti the then–Democratic candidate at the time, John Kerry. Though the event wasn't billed as such, the real issue was who was the more pro-life of the two candidates. Though neither candidate was explicitly named, it was John Kerry's Catholicism that was being called into question. The C-Span cameras recorded the message and played it the whole next week on U.S. television. So the explicit material was not on the election as such but on whether a Catholic could be soft about pro-life and liberal about abortion. The talks given by men (with the happy exception of John Langan, SJ) were unforgiving of any ambiguity about the matter. Monika's was the last talk.

She pointedly recommended that "we stop being a church of condemnations and concentrate on being a church of engagement." She did not mention her own engagement with unwanted children nor her adoption of three African-American children. She sought to widen the lens of the onlookers and recommended a "respect for life that involves growth in empathy, compassion, forgiveness, reconciliation, solidarity, and always preferential attention to the weakest and the most vulnerable in the economy as well as the vulnerable in the womb (the two categories overlap)." She did not mention her monthly overnight volunteer stays in a homeless shelter for women; she did not mention how concretely she identified with such a population. (How she had time to invest herself with the weakest and most vulnerable in her neighborhood is amazing, given the demands on her both nationally and internationally with all the duties of the presidency of the Association of Catholic Colleges and Universities.)

It was notable how her remarks were greeted with a complete and sullen silence. Her listeners had previously shown much enthusiasm for the speakers who were conceptually clear about conception and absolute about the evil of its eradication.

I doubt Monika would have developed the three qualities I have mentioned in this article had her intelligence been of a lesser quality. But even her intelligence needed a center; otherwise it would become a fissiparous mélange of this and that, a mindless, liberal relativism. The center for Monika was her Catholic faith. In her seven-decade lifetime she inhabited it more and more fully. As it kept developing, she developed along with it. She came to appropriate her own faith by daily prayer, regular attendance at the sacraments, the Eucharist in particular. The enlargement of her mind and heart reveals the theological adage about the *lex orandi* generating the *lex credendi*, the rule of prayer guiding the rule of beliefs.

Those of us who knew Monika well were constantly impressed by her virtue of reverence for others. I have seen this virtue operating toward bishops and theologians—even with those with whom she vigorously disagreed. It was striking to learn from her children at her wake that she never talked religion to them until and unless they had asked her a question about it. Such was her trust of God's co-laboring in them and her reverence for them developmentally. She also grew all her life in her reverence for God. The realm of transcendence was not vacated by the realm of theory growing in her. She gave them both their due because interiority was the castle to which she repaired with constancy. And raising three children ensured that all four realms of meaning were alive and active in this wonderfully whole human being.

I have mentioned her reverence as a virtue but I wouldn't finish the story if I didn't include the category that was most intriguing to her in her last few years. This was the theological implications of virtue. She couldn't wait to be relieved of her presidential responsibilities at the Association of Catholic Colleges and Universities after nine years so she could write about "the virtues." She became a member of the Woodstock Theological Center just a few months before she died. The night before her cerebral hemorrhage she penned an outline of the book she had in mind to write. It was titled *The Fullness of Life*. It was to have been about the three virtues of faith, hope, and love. What is eerie, to say the least, about her e-mail to me was her addendum: "I have set no time limits for completing this work." Indeed, we can piously surmise, she's still at it.

[A] redemptive life is one that continually reaches out to the coming of God's reign in human affairs. That means change—quite profound change in many of the ways we treat one another both individually and through the social structures that control relationships and opportunities. There is nothing in our human experiences and activities and organizations that is not relevant to the reign of God. It is the reign of God in all creation that is the hope and goal of Christian life. And the coming of the reign of God is the reordering of all creation within the hospitality of its Creator.

— from *Guests of God:*
Stewards of Divine Creation
by Monika K. Hellwig

Chapter 7

Monika Hellwig, Parishioner

Suzanne Clark[1]

To the people of the parish of St. Rose of Lima in Gaithersburg, Maryland, and their pastor, Reverend Robert D. Duggan, this book is dedicated in gratitude for the experience of Christian community that they have afforded me.

—Monika Hellwig, *Guests of God*

The last time I saw Monika, I was standing at her bedside in the Washington Hospital Center, the day following the aneurysm that was to take her life. In a deep coma from which she never awakened, her breathing—slow, rhythmic, and deep—made an indelible impression on me. The gentle rise and fall of her chest—the breath of life so effortlessly inhaled, so peacefully exhaled—is an image that returns to me daily in my practices of yoga and meditation. As I try to center myself by focusing on my own breathing, I nearly always lovingly recall and cherish that image of Monika breathing so peacefully, patiently awaiting the Lord's final call.

The first time I saw Monika, I was standing in the foyer of the Parish Centre at St. Rose as I routinely did, greeting parishioners arriving for Sunday Mass. Our pastor, Fr. Bob Duggan, who also had the custom of standing at the front door to greet folks as they arrived, had been

1. Thanks to Fr. Robert Duggan for his help in assembling and editing this material.

85

speaking with her for a few minutes and then brought her over to introduce her to me. "Sue, this is Monika Hellwig, and she has just moved into the parish. Why don't you show her around?" It was a familiar hand-off, one he had done countless times before, and I always delighted in my role of getting to know the newcomers and making them feel immediately welcome. "And you are *the* Monika Hellwig?" I wanted to say, but it was clear that this was not someone who sought or wanted special attention. So we chatted for a few minutes, and then I introduced her to a longtime parishioner, someone I knew would sit with her at Mass and continue to make her feel at home.

I asked Fr. Duggan if he recalled that first meeting with Monika at the parish. "Yes, I do," he assured me. "I had met her over dinner in her apartment in Georgetown almost twenty years earlier through a mutual acquaintance, but our paths had not crossed in the meantime. She didn't recall that first meeting with me, but with a smile and a twinkle in her eye, she asked me what she had served for dinner that evening. When she said she had just moved into the parish boundaries and would like to register, I was of course delighted and told her she would be most welcome. She also said she would like to get involved in the life of the parish. I told her to give me a call, and I would be very happy to discuss it with her. I was amazed when she called me later that same week, repeating her offer. When we did sit down to talk several weeks later, it was clear to me that she really did want to be involved 'in whatever way would be most helpful,' as she put it. I gave her our 'Opportunity Knocks' time and talent booklet and suggested she look it over for what interested her, but I did point out some of the possibilities where I thought her talents might best be used—as part of our ongoing adult lecture series, or perhaps in one of our evangelization ministries— RCIA, Another Look [for returning Catholics], or Ministry to the Baptized [for Catholics and other Christians completing initiation]. I recall very clearly, as she was getting up to leave she said, 'You know, I've lived in many parishes in the archdiocese over the past thirty years, and I have made it a point always to register and always to offer to help out in any way the pastor wished. You are the first pastor who has ever accepted my invitation.' I was stunned and saddened, and to tell the truth I don't remember how I responded other than to say that I would truly be delighted to have her involved at St. Rose."[2]

2. Fr. Robert Duggan, interview by author, Gaithersburg, Maryland, 31 May 2009.

And get involved she did. Despite Monika's international stature as a theologian, her devotion to her family, and the many demands of her professional life, she was neither too important nor too busy to be active as a parishioner at St. Rose. It was our custom to provide the opportunity for newcomers to register in the parish at a monthly gathering, where a brief video was shown, staff members and parish leaders introduced themselves, and materials were given out that described the parish and how to get involved. Together with the census form that was the official way to register in the parish, we offered an optional Covenant Statement—an invitation to intentional discipleship that included commitments to worship regularly with the community, to embrace our understanding of stewardship by making gifts of time, talent, and treasure, and to become an active participant in the life of the parish family as one's particular circumstances allowed. Monika's Covenant Statement, signed on 14 May 1994, remains in the parish archives today, a relic of a committed relationship destined to bring countless blessings to the people of St. Rose, but also to afford Monika the richly meaningful "experience of Christian community" to which she alludes in the book dedication quoted at the beginning of this chapter.

Ministry of the Word

I believe one of Monika's most cherished ministries was her role as lector every third week at the 9:00 a.m. Mass. Her cultured British accent and strong proclamation of the text was appreciated by all who heard her, and for the majority of parishioners this was the primary setting in which she was known. Those who ministered with her had the opportunity to experience something of the depth of learning and spirituality she brought to that ministry. It is a requirement at St. Rose that all who proclaim the Scriptures at the weekend Masses gather on Saturday morning to receive some exegetical background on the text, to pray and do faith-sharing, and then to rehearse and offer one another suggestions about how best to proclaim the text.

John Carson, who served on the same team as Monika, offered the following observations: "The three teams gathered in the chapel on the Saturday morning preceding the weekend services at which the respective team would be proclaiming the Scriptures. Someone would have prepared a commentary on the Scriptures to be proclaimed, giving a bit of exegesis and tying the three readings together so that we would be aware of how our selection integrated with the others. On the Saturdays when that task fell to Monika, I knew I was in for a treat, a stellar 'breaking open' of the Word. And when it was my turn to lead, if I blundered or misspoke or fudged she would make corrections in such a way that, even though she flatly contradicted my statement, I felt pleased to have been so 'close,' even from left field. She had a teaching charism I don't think I've experienced ever before or since."[3]

Another lector, Beverly Hawkins, shared her recollection of those Saturday morning formation sessions: "She brought intellectual insight and history to our focus on the readings, but what REALLY touched me was her humility in sharing her depth of knowledge. I remember once, for example, that a member of our team was explaining some historical point (I don't remember what it was) and what the person was saying was actually incorrect. Monika clarified the history point, but her effort, in word and demeanor, was much less directed to the point of history than to compassion and gentleness to the member of our team. Additionally, she made sure that the REAL point was not the history, but the movement God wants in our hearts. It was insightful, lovely and I'll never forget it."[4]

John Carson also made reference to Monika's humility. "I met her for the first time, at St. Rose of Lima. I was awestruck; she was, well, Monika. She quickly put me at ease, and when I mentioned how I had heard of her so many years ago, she thanked me and made me feel as though she was honored to meet me! . . . More than her learning, which was vast; more than her generosity, which flowed freely; more than any other virtue I associate with Monika was her humility."[5]

Fr. Duggan was convinced of the need for voices other than his to be heard, and so on occasion he would invite Monika to share a "catechetical reflection" at Sunday Eucharist. Careful to observe the letter of the law, Fr. Duggan would tell the assembly that he was about to give a homily—which then lasted about thirty seconds or less. Afterwards he would observe that as a laywoman, Monika, who was "merely" baptized, was not allowed to preach, but that she had agreed to offer a

3. John Carson, e-mail communication to author, 28 May 2009.
4. Beverly Hawkins, e-mail communication to author, 28 May 2009.
5. John Carson, 28 May 2009.

catechetical reflection on the word. Her reflection was always elegant and simple, profound yet accessible.

Fr. Duggan recalls his experience of having her both as a proclaimer of the word and as one who listened regularly to his own preaching. "Of all the homily guides that I used in my thirty-five-plus years of preaching, hers[6] was the one that I would, time and again, find the most insightful and spiritually nourishing. I would sometimes ask myself, 'How can I use this material now, knowing she'll be there and hear what a poor job I do of capturing the depth of her insights?' But I knew she listened without judgment for whatever of value the Spirit managed to let escape my lips. Occasionally—not often, but on occasion—she would come up to me after Mass and tell me that I had given a really good homily. Since she regularly heard me preach and only occasionally said that, I knew that my other efforts were merely adequate."[7]

Evangelization and Catechetical Ministries

One of the ministries to which Monika was most devoted was our outreach to returning Catholics, called Another Look. We advertised regularly that every Thursday evening inactive Catholics could "drop in" to talk about the issues that concerned them. The numbers were always small, and some would come only a time or two, while others might stay for months. But Monika never gave a hint that she felt she was wasting her time for so small a number. On the contrary, she seemed grateful to be allowed to minister in so intimate a way with people probing the meaning of faith in their lives.

John Carson speaks of how privileged he felt to share responsibility for facilitating sessions with Monika. Again he offers his perspective: "Occasionally people would come to a session with an ugly chip on their shoulder, because of some real or imagined (more often, real) hurt inflicted on them by 'Holy Mother Church.' Monika would listen attentively, engage them in conversation, agree that their hurts were very painful, give examples of similar instances she was aware of, and how she and others were dealing with the pain. These people knew they had

---

6. Monika K. Hellwig, *Gladness Their Escort: Homiletic Reflections for Sundays and Feastdays* (Collegeville, MN: Liturgical Press, 1990).

7. Fr. Robert Duggan, e-mail communication to author, 28 June 2009.

been heard, validated, and even if they were not changed, they were far more at peace. I remember one series of sessions with a couple who had left the Church years ago, and were feeling much more comfortable in the Episcopal faith tradition. In the end, Monika suggested that they both continue that path, since it seemed to her that was where God wanted them. . . . Then there were evenings when no one showed up, and I had Monika all to myself. So many questions, and Monika received them all, and gave me the benefit of not only her learning, but her wisdom."[8]

Monika also helped facilitate our Ministry to the Baptized process. This was a group for those who were seeking admission to the Catholic Church but who were already catechized sufficiently that they did not belong in the RCIA process. The richness of her knowledge of theology and church history stunned these folks who were interested in becoming Catholics, and few were ever aware of the stature of this woman who was so unassuming and patient in answering their questions. Paul Riekhof was one of those fortunate enough to know Monika in that setting.

> When I first met Monika, through the Ministry to the Baptized, I was not privy to the lore surrounding her theological background and knowledge. She was introduced to us in a casual way that indicated that she had helpful subject matter knowledge and was a professor of theology, but not much else. However, it became clear in about thirty seconds of listening to her that she was an exceptional scholar who not only knew a great many things, as all scholars do, but who also had the ability to impart her wisdom to others in terms that anyone could understand; and she seemed to be able to do this with almost no effort whatsoever. Through her, we were able to gain knowledge and perspective on the issues we discussed at levels not often encountered, in my experience, in a local church setting. It was a great privilege!
>
> Even better yet, there were no airs with Monika. She always seemed very down to earth to me. During run of the mill conversations, she would comport herself in a manner that would never make you guess (or feel) that she was an internationally recognized scholar. She did not appear to have any difficulty relating to people on the human level which in my experience can be a problem for

8. John Carson, 28 May 2009.

some academics. She served on the same lector team as Maria [my wife] for many years. So Maria knew her as well and the three of us chatted from time to time. I recall one Sunday after Mass when Monika, Maria, Willa, Ian [our children] and I all sat down in front of the PC [Parish Centre] to talk. The kids, who were very young at the time, were eating doughnuts, playing and engaging in the conversation at points. I remember being struck by how well she interacted with the kids. She very easily communicated on their level and was playful with them. For some reason this surprised me. Probably because by then I was fairly well-versed in "who" Monika was on the international theological scene and as a result had incorporated some academic stereotypes in my point of view. But she did not seem to have any such bias in her. She was a down to earth member of the parish that day and most likely every day.[9]

Yet another way in which Monika ministered was as a speaker at our adult education lecture series. Accustomed as she was to drawing crowds of hundreds to her speaking engagements, she never gave the slightest hint that it was beneath her to speak to the much smaller gatherings that might show up for a talk on a Wednesday evening in Lent. One evening in 2003, her topic was "Authority in the Church Today." Her description in the flyer describing her talk said:

> How does discernment of the will of God relate to hierarchic authority in the Church? Who has authority in the Church, and in what matters?
>
> How does one assess the truth and extent of claims of authority?
>
> When does obedience to authority become an invalid excuse for failure to take responsibility for discerning and acting? What obedience is appropriate to well-informed adults? Does disapproval of an action by church authority always mean the action is wrong and the doer is sinning?
>
> What does God really want us to do, and how can we know?

Needless to say, parishioners came to realize the treasure in our midst, and she developed a number of devoted followers.

Carol Lechner was one of those parishioners who listened when Monika spoke:

9. Paul Riekhof, e-mail communication to author, 9 June 2009.

I recall one talk on small Christian communities during which Monika said that being a member of a small Christian community within the context of a larger Catholic community was essential for her life as a Catholic. She affirmed the central role that small faith communities have played in the life of St. Rose of Lima, connecting parishioners one by one and in turn to the entire body.

By far for me the most profound reflection that Monika gave at St. Rose occurred in March of 2005, just months before her death. This was Monika's final formal address to us and the topic during that Lenten season was Eucharist.

I remember feeling deeply moved by this Lenten reflection because it was clear that Monika was speaking about the experience of Eucharist that she had come to know as a member of our parish. She had found in St. Rose, and helped nurture by virtue of her abiding presence, a Body of Christ that was the kind of Catholic community that Vatican II paved the way for. For me, Monika's death was a profound loss, both personally but especially for St. Rose. In addition to being able to tell our story in the beautiful way that she told it on March 2, 2005, she embodied deep commitment to a flawed church and unfailing resolve to challenge it to grow. And as a woman, she was our beloved female priest.[10]

Gardens and Grounds

Perhaps my favorite memory of Monika is seeing how much she enjoyed tending the parish grounds as a member of our Gardens and Grounds Committee. Twice yearly—spring and fall—we would hold Shape-Up Day, inviting parishioners to turn out in great numbers on a Saturday to help care for the extensive landscaping on the parish property. Monika loved gardening and she could be seen trimming the long expanse of forsythia bushes in front of the Historic Chapel, or crawling on her hands and knees to weed the flower patches at the entrance to the Parish Centre. Monika Hellwig, internationally respected theologian, was not above getting her hands dirty! Plans are unfolding for a landscape memorial on parish grounds as a tribute to this special but humble and unpretentious woman.

10. Carol Lechner, e-mail communication to author, 6 June 2009.

Spiritual Pilgrim

Those of us who came to know Monika as a fellow parishioner were certainly aware of her immense learning and her international renown. But we met on common ground as members of a pilgrim people. Some of us had the opportunity to come to know her on a more personal level, as a mother worried about her children, as someone who was concerned about having sufficient financial resources to meet sizeable family medical bills, as a Vatican II Catholic challenged to be at home in what seemed increasingly like a church in retreat from the council's call for *aggiornamento*.

Fr. Duggan served as Monika's regular confessor and spiritual director for a number of years, a ministry that he describes as particularly humbling. "Every priest comes to know the 'secrets of the heart' of an incredibly broad range of people—simple souls of stunning holiness, surprising stories of people who wrestle with demons of sin and addiction and guilt and tragic loss. Over a lifetime of ministry, there are hundreds and even thousands for whom a priest plays an intimate role on their spiritual pilgrimage. Some of those people have left me feeling grateful for what God has spared me; others, I have envied for the extraordinary graces with which they have been blessed. The feeling I most associate with my role as Monika's confessor and spiritual director is that of being an unworthy instrument of God's grace and hoping so very much that I would not stand in the way of what God was doing in her life. I think I can relate to how some of those confessors must have felt who ministered to St. Teresa of Avila."[11]

Monika's position as president of the Association of Catholic Colleges and Universities required her to be deeply involved in negotiations with church leaders in this country and in the Vatican over how the apostolic constitution *Ex Corde Ecclesiae* would be interpreted and implemented. Fr. Duggan recalls conversations with her about her involvement in the back-and-forth struggle to reach an agreement viable for the American scene yet still acceptable to the Vatican. "I was intrigued to understand more deeply how she managed to keep her spirits up when she was dealing with a side of the hierarchical Church that was often anything but edifying. I asked her how she could be so sanguine

11. Fr. Robert Duggan, e-mail communication to author, 2 June 2009.

at times when it seemed that Vatican II's promise of renewal was being systematically undermined by curial bureaucrats. Her response was a mixture of a sophisticated, nuanced understanding that situated the present moment in a broad historical perspective, combined with an absolutely simple faith in the Spirit's presence in the Church—simple in the most profound sense of the word. Her spirituality was so bedrock traditional, so simple, that it was stunning."[12]

My Last Conversation with Monika

St. Rose has long had a tradition of gathering in the fall for what we call our "Fiesta," a community-building and fund-raising event that concludes with a lively outdoor liturgy, all of which takes many months of preparation and hundreds of helping hands to support. Monika had not previously been involved in Fiesta due to her extensive professional commitments. But she had recently (and at long last) retired, and so it was that on 24 September 2005, I ran into Monika in the foyer of the Parish Centre, where our huge flea market was teeming with bargain hunters. Little did I know that this was to be my last conversation with her, as it was just six days before her death.

The parish at that time was experiencing the pains and challenges of a transition in pastoral leadership. The pastor of almost twenty years had recently retired and the new pastor, not yet reconciled to having been transferred from the parish he had founded more than twenty years before, was struggling to cope with the much different kind of community that he found at St. Rose. Monika was keenly aware of the tensions and complexities involved in such a major pastoral change. We sat and talked together at some length about what was happening, and in her typically wise and thoughtful way, she shared her perspective and expressed the hope that things would not change too quickly. She told me of her concern, and hope, that the deeply held and cherished vision statement of the parish (*In Christ, we are bread for one another: Broken. . . we gather. Nourished. . . we reach out*) not only continue to guide the community's life but also flourish under the new leadership. Monika had found a home in our faith community and she joined us in living that vision; she contributed to the care with which we prepared

12. Ibid.

for and celebrated liturgy; she promoted respect for and empowerment of lay leadership; she exemplified commitment to authentic solidarity with the poor and those so often marginalized by the church itself.

As I reflect now on that precious last conversation, I realize that she had found at St. Rose something of the vision of church that she spent her entire adult life promoting: as both a renowned theologian and as an "ordinary" parish member, she had championed the implementation of Vatican II with its recognition of the rights and responsibilities of the People of God, baptized and called to live as priest, prophet, and king. By her matter-of-fact way of becoming involved in our parish, she put flesh onto an ecclesiology that theologians often portray, but do not always live in so personal a fashion. The church of Vatican II was part of her DNA, and Monika humbly, generously, and intentionally nurtured its growth in the community of St. Rose of Lima.

I look back with gratitude on that last, inspiring hour I shared with Monika, and I pray that sharing it and stories of her life as a parishioner will offer to others some measure of the hope that her memory continues to offer me.

I have fixed my eyes on your hills, Jerusalem, my destiny.
Though I cannot see the end for me, I cannot turn away.
We have set our hearts for the way;
this journey is our destiny.
Let no one walk alone.
The journey makes us one.

> —from "Jerusalem, My Destiny" by Rory Cooney,
> which was sung at Monika's funeral

Copyright © 1990 by GIA Publications, Inc., 7404 S. Mason Ave., Chicago, IL 60638.
www.giamusic.com. 800.442.1358. All rights reserved. Used by permission.

Books by Monika Hellwig

What Are the Theologians Saying? Pflaum, 1970.

The Meaning of the Sacraments. Pflaum, 1972.

The Christian Creeds: A Faith to Live By. Pflaum/Standard, 1973.

Tradition: The Catholic Story Today. Pflaum/Standard, 1975.

The Eucharist and the Hunger of the World. Paulist Press, 1976; 2nd edition Sheed & Ward, 1992.

What Are They Saying about Death and Christian Hope? Paulist Press, 1978.

Understanding Catholicism. Paulist Press, 1981.

Whose Experience Counts in Theological Reflection? Marquette University Press, 1982.

Sign of Reconciliation and Conversion. Michael Glazier, Inc., 1982.

Jesus, the Compassion of God: New Perspectives on the Tradition of Christianity. Michael Glazier, Inc., 1983.

Theology as a Fine Art. Pamphlet. Michael Glazier, Inc., 1983.

Christian Women in a Troubled World. Paulist Press, 1985.

Gladness Their Escort: Homiletic Reflections, Years A, B, and C. Michael Glazier, 1987.

The Role of the Theologian. Pamphlet. Sheed & Ward, 1987.

Catholic Faith and Contemporary Questions. Pamphlet. University of Tulsa, 1988.

Death or Dialogue? From the Age of Monologue to the Age of Dialogue. Coauthored with Leonard Swidler, John Cobb, and Paul Knitter. Trinity Press International, 1990.

Journey of Hope and Grace: Advent 1990. Coauthored with Mary Lou Kownacki. Pax Christi, 1990.

A Case for Peace in Reason and Faith. Liturgical Press, 1992.

What Are the Theologians Saying Now? Christian Classics, 1992.

A Catholic Scholar's Journey through the Twentieth Century. University of Dayton, 1993 Marianist Lecture.

The Modern Catholic Encyclopedia, Coedited with Michael Glazier. Liturgical Press, 1994.

Guests of God: Stewards of Divine Creation. Paulist Press, 2000.

Continuing the Journey: Celebrating 40 Years of Vatican II. Coauthored with Jacquie Jambor, Robert Blair Kaiser, and Nathan Mitchell, et al. Thomas More Association, 2002.

Public Dimensions of a Believer's Life: Rediscovering the Cardinal Virtues. Rowman & Littlefield Publishers, Inc., 2005.

Original Selfishness: Original Sin and Evil in the Light of Evolution. Coauthored with Daryl P. Domning. Ashgate Science and Religion, 2006.

---

* Readers may also wish to consult the Catholic Periodical and Literature Index database, put out by the Catholic college and university libraries. This database is continually being updated; a recent search for Monika Hellwig's name yielded 140 sources.

Events in Monika Hellwig's Life

1929	Born December 10 in Breslau, Germany; the family later moves to Holland
1940	Moves to Scotland with her two sisters after Hitler invades Holland
1949	Receives law degree from the University of Liverpool
1951	Receives social science degree from the University of Liverpool
1952	Joins the Society of Catholic Medical Missionaries
1956	Receives master's degree in theology from The Catholic University of America in Washington DC
1963–66	Works in Rome during Second Vatican Council; during this time she is released from her religious vows
1967	Begins teaching at Georgetown University in Washington DC
1968	Receives PhD in theology from The Catholic University of America
1970	Publishes her first book, *What Are the Theologians Saying?*
1970	Adopts Erica, eleven months old
1974	Adopts Michael, two and one half years old

1980   Adopts Carlos, six years old

1984   Honored with John Courtney Murray Award by Catholic
                Theological Society of America

1985   Delivers first Madaleva Lecture in Spirituality at Saint
                Mary's College, South Bend, Indiana

1986   Elected president of the Catholic Theological Society of
                America

1990   Named Landegger Distinguished Professor of Theology
                at Georgetown University

1994   Registers as a parishioner at St. Rose of Lima Catholic
                Church in Gaithersburg, Maryland

1996–2005   Retires from Georgetown University to serve as execu-
                tive director of the Association of Catholic Colleges and
                Universities

2005   Retires from Association of Catholic Colleges and
                Universities; is appointed senior fellow at Woodstock
                Theological Center. Dies September 30.

Index